GOD'S STORIES

AS TOLD BY GOD'S CHILDREN

ADULTS' EDITION

THE BIBLE
FOR NORMAL PEOPLE

THE BIBLE
FOR NORMAL PEOPLE

Library of Congress Control Number available on request.

ISBN: 978-1-964423-27-2 (Print)

ISBN: 978-1-964423-28-9 (eBook)

TABLE OF CONTENTS

1 Preface to Adults' Edition

2 Introduction

4 In the Beginning... *René August*

7 Eden *Jared Byas*

10 In Our Image *Mari Jørstad*

15 Re-Creation *Jonathan Lewis-Jong*

18 A Wandering Aramean *Lauren O'Connell*

21 Hey There, Stranger *Carolyn Custis James*

24 A Family Affair *Sarah Shectman*

27 Israel, Is It? *Rachel Starr*

30 Here Comes the Dreamer *Safwat Marzouk*

33 Here I Am *Chauncey Diego Francisco Handy*

36 By This They Will Know *Brent A. Strawn*

39 Rules to Love By *Brent A. Strawn*

42 Home *Mark Brett*

45 When Judges Judged *Erin H. Moon*

48 The People Want a King *Cynthia Shafer-Elliott*

51 Every King Needs a Prophet *Ellen Davis & Morley van Yperen*

53 Proverbial Animal Farm *Katharine Dell*

56 A Kingdom Divided *Dan McClellan*

59 Here Comes Trouble *Deborah Winters*

62 You Want Me to Do What?! *Jione Havea*

65 Here Comes Trouble...Again *Anna Sieges Beal*

68 For I Know the Plans *Alexiana Fry*

71 Are You There, God? *Joshua James*

74 With Friends Like These *Katharine Dell*

77 Days Like These *Peter Enns*

79 Home, Again *Steed Vernyl Davidson*

82 Who Is In & Who Is Out? *Aaron Higashi*

84 The Faithful Foreign Woman *Havilah Dharamraj*

87 For Such a Time as This *Monica J. Melanchthon*

90 In the Lions' Den *Brian Fiu Kolia*

93 Even More Trouble *Shayna Sheinfeld*

96 On the Road to Damascus *Sarah Emanuel*

99 The Story Collectors *Isaac T. Soon*

102 Mary's Song *Jennifer Garcia Bashaw*

105 Welcome, Baby Jesus *Shannon K. Evans*

108 Leading the Way *Tamice Spencer-Helms*

111 The Sermon on the Mount *Shane Claiborne*

114 Seeing Jesus *Elizabeth Enns Petters*

117 Through the Roof *Kylie Crabbe*

120 Get Up! *Summer Kinard*

123 By a Well *Jennifer T. Kaalund*

126 They Were Satisfied *Meredith J. C. Warren*

129 What Kind of Man? *Camille Szramiak Arneberg*

132 Hey There, Neighbor *Shane Claiborne*

135 What is Better? *Marika Rose*

138 Rejoice with Me *Savannah Locke*

141 It Ain't Fair *Miguel A. De La Torre*

144 Making Things Right *Raj Nadella*

147 A Very Big Party *Richard Rohr*

150 A Funny Kind of King *Jarrod McKenna*

153 Do This & Remember *Marlena Graves*

156 Gethsemane *Bradley Jersak*

158 My God, My God *Drew G. I. Hart*

160 Do Not Be Afraid *Elizabeth Schrader Polczer*

163 A Mighty Wind *Jennifer Garcia Bashaw*

166 Everyone's Invited *Rachel Mann*

169 A Revelation *Terry J. Stokes*

172 A New Heaven & A New Earth *Randy Woodley*

174 Now What?

243 Glossary

245 Authors

PREFACE TO ADULTS' EDITION

In April 2024, The Bible for Normal People launched a Kickstarter to fund an illustrated children's storybook Bible: *God's Stories as told by God's Children*. The concept was both simple and revolutionary: to create a children's Bible not just informed by the best in biblical scholarship, but one that introduced kids to basic concepts in biblical scholarship *and* retold key biblical narratives in playful, biblically faithful ways.

We wanted to create a children's Bible that did not hide the Bible's weird bits, but embraced them. That did not gloss over repetition or discrepancies in the biblical texts, but used them to show kids the Bible's human fingerprints. We wanted kids to know that how the Bible works tells us as much about who God is as what the Bible says, and that reading the Bible should be the beginning of a conversation, not the end of one. And while we may have used kid-friendly terms such as "voices" rather than "source criticism," and "ancient ways of storytelling" rather than "literary criticism," the essentials are the same.

If you're excited just reading this, it will come as no surprise to you that the Kickstarter we launched was a *smashing* success. It did, however, come as a surprise to us. We knew we were on to a good thing—we were creating a storybook Bible that we would read to our own children and grandchildren, but let's be honest for a second here: we love talking about the Bible and that's why people avoid us at parties. So, who knew whether this would resonate with normal (i.e., *not* us) people around the world?

But here's the most surprising thing about the Kickstarter campaign: so many of you wanted this book for yourselves. Not for your kids or your grandkids or your nieces or your nephews or your friend's kids, but for you. For the kid you used to be. The one who had all the questions and nowhere to ask them. Who saw the narrative wrinkles and was told to ignore them. Who wrestled with the biblical texts and was labeled a troublemaker (or worse).

So here it is: the original text of *God's Stories as told by God's Children* (minus the illustrations and the Let's Talk questions), repackaged in an adult-friendly format for those of you who needed this book when you were a kid.

Thanks for joining us on this journey: we are so glad you are here.

INTRODUCTION

Before you begin your adventure through these pages—before you meet the kings and queens, tricksters and tax collectors, prophets and poets that pepper its pages—there is something you should know.

The Bible is weird.

There. We said it. But maybe you already know this. Maybe you've heard the Garden of Eden story and thought, "Huh…snakes don't talk…weird." Or maybe you've heard about Noah and the flood and wondered, "How'd Noah get all those animals on one boat…weird." Or maybe you've heard stories about Jesus and thought, "People can't walk on water…weird." So, we agree: the Bible is weird.

But why is it so weird?

That is a very good question. The Bible is weird because the Bible is old. Not old like a grandpa, but really old. Ancient, even. Can you count to 100? How about 1,000? Well keep counting, because the Bible was written thousands of years ago. Back before books or cars or buttons or guns or phones or even underpants had been invented.

Because the Bible is old, there are going to be stories in here that seem scary or strange or harsh or silly or just plain weird. Some stories might leave you with more questions than answers. Old stories from ancient times didn't always follow the same storytelling rules that we have today. So if you are reading something and it sounds weird, remember—things written thousands of years ago might sound weird to people today. And that's okay! Because the Bible is ancient and we are not.

The Bible is weird because it has many storytellers.

The Bible was written by lots of people. We can't tell you exactly how many because nobody knows for sure, but we do know that it was a lot. But what's really fun is that these people did not know they were writing the Bible, because when the Bible was being written, the Bible hadn't been invented yet.

What?! Weird. Let us explain.

"The Bible" is not one book. The Bible is made up of many books. And these many books are made up of many stories and laws and prophecies and songs and teachings and other kinds of ancient storytelling.

The stories we find in our Bibles today were very special to ancient Jews and, later, Christians, especially when times were hard. Through them, they could see God at work in their worlds. So they gathered these many writings together and retold them in and for their own times and places.

But before that—before they were gathered together—these stories were special to the people who told them and heard them, and the people who wrote them and copied them, over and over. These storytellers were often very different from one another. They lived in different times and places. They believed different things. Sometimes, they even disagreed with one another!

Because the Bible's stories are told by many storytellers, the books that make up the Bible can sound different from one another. *God's Stories as told by God's Children* also has many storytellers—just like a grownup's Bible. As you are reading this book, you might think, "This story sounds and feels different from the one before it," and you would be right! When the stories of the Bible were gathered together, the many different voices of the storytellers were kept, so the Bible—and this book—sound like many conversations.

These are the conversations you are invited into today.

So, as you read through this book, remember:

Your voice is important.
Your questions are important.
Your thoughts and your feelings as you read through these stories are important.
The conversations you have about these stories are important.

Because the Bible shows us that many voices are needed to tell God's stories …including yours.

JEREMIAH 29:1-14

The one that begins where you'd least expect

IN THE BEGINNING

As told by René August

Imagine that you live in the city of Jerusalem. Not the Jerusalem of today, with its cars and phones and internet, but the Jerusalem of long, long ago—the Jerusalem of 586 BCE.

This is the time of the prophet Jeremiah and the mighty, scary Babylonian Empire.

Are you ready to travel back to that time? To visit the Jerusalem of 2,500 years ago? We must warn you—it might be scary. But this is where our stories begin: with a big, bad army, a city on fire, and a people who have to leave everything they have ever known behind. Everything, that is, except their stories.

So take a deep breath for courage—are you ready? Alright, let's go…

****

You wake to the sounds of screaming. "It's happening!" Your family members call out to each other in panicked voices. The Babylonian soldiers who have surrounded your city for more than two years are here. They have finally broken through Jerusalem's walls.

You make your way to the north end of the city. The city gates are burning! The city's leaders and teachers (the ones who remember the stories, traditions, and history) are calling for calm. But who can be calm? Everywhere you look, everything you once held dear is reduced to ash and rubble.

The priests and others are praying in the temple. People are gathering their families and possessions, desperate to save them from the fires that are burning everywhere.

Soldiers scream and point at you, and you realize that you need to move toward the East Gate, the mighty gate that once offered assurance and protection.

It is noisy and confusing, and you cannot find your family. Soldiers on either side move you into rows of five or six, guiding you away from the city.

You turn your head back for one last look at Jerusalem. Even the temple where you worshipped God is burning!

"The priests said this would never happen," you think to yourself. "The prophets told us there would always be a king descended from David on the throne."

The sun begins to set. The soldiers force you to stop and rest for the night. They stand all around you, ensuring there is no escape.

The priests gather the people for prayers. To worship the God who allowed the Babylonian armies to destroy Jerusalem and take the people from their homes. The God who left everyone so disappointed.

Will you join them as they pray?

As the sun greets the morning, you realize you have never been this far from home. The soldiers demand you keep moving. With tired body and aching feet, you walk. You pass some of the mighty "prophets" who said this would never happen: "God would never allow it!" Yet, here you all are.

What will you say to them?

After weeks of walking, the soldiers seem excited. Their pace quickens. You look ahead and realize that before the sun sets, you will be in Babylon. The city of your captors. As you arrive in the city, the gate closes behind you and the soldiers walk away. Some people begin making shelters, others go exploring. Still others sit weeping.

What will you do?

You have now lived a month in this strange new city. You are tired of waiting for God to act. To make a way home for you. And now a letter will be read from Jerusalem from the prophet Jeremiah. Jeremiah, who warned of this day. Jeremiah, whom no one listened to. The letter will be read at sunset under the big willow tree beside the river.

"To all of the people taken from Jerusalem to Babylon," Jeremiah writes, "Build houses and live in them. Plant gardens and eat what they grow. Seek peace for the city you have been exiled to. Pray to the LORD for it, for as good things happen to the city, good things will happen to you. For the LORD says, 'When 70 years have passed, I will bring you back to the place I have promised. I will gather you from all the places I have sent you and will restore you to the place I have exiled you from.'"

Around you, people are weeping. The wait has only just begun…
What will you do?

The Beginnings of the Bible

The earliest bits of the Bible began as songs and oral stories, passed from one person to another from memory. Later bits of the Bible were written on scrolls—scribes in palaces recorded laws and important events, students of prophets wrote down their teachings, and priests composed prayers and liturgies.

This writing and storytelling happened in lots of different places for many different reasons. As the years passed, these writings and stories were copied over and over by scribes who updated older texts for their place and time, adding new bits and deleting those they did not need.

After the Babylonians destroyed Jerusalem and took the people into exile (to live in lands far from their homes), scribes began gathering these writings and stories.

And these scribes had some big questions. Questions like: Who are we as a people, now that we have no king and no temple to unite us? Why do bad things happen? And where is God when they do?!

These questions influenced the writings they gathered and shaped how they put them all together. Over many years of gathering and copying, these writings began to look like the Bible we know today.

So the Bible kind of began in exile, which is why this book begins with the exile. Because these questions and this experience shaped the Bibles we have today.

The one where God creates

EDEN

As told by Jared Byas

———————

After Jeremiah's letter was read, we looked at each other with wide eyes. Sensing it was time, the elders gathered all of us children near. Their voices were warm and kind as they began to tell us the stories of our ancestors—God's stories.

Miriam, the oldest of the elders, began, brushing her silver hair from her eyes. "This reminds me of the time when the LORD God built the world."

"Oh yes," Samuel nodded. "Have we told you that story before? No? Well get ready, because it's a good one."

"Once upon a time, the earth was a total mess," Miriam began. "There were no trees to climb and no friends to climb them with. Just a dry and dusty wasteland. But then, water started to bubble up from the *adamah*—the ground—turning that dust into soft, squishy mud. And the LORD God, like a very talented artist, took this mud and carefully shaped it into an *adam*—a human. When the LORD God was done, the LORD God breathed life into it."

Samuel continued. "The LORD God planted a beautiful garden in the east, probably not too far from here, in a place called Eden." Samuel drew an invisible map of the garden with his fingers in the air. "In this garden," he said, "there were two special trees: the tree of life and the tree of the knowledge of good and evil. The LORD God put the first human in this garden to take care of it and made just one rule: 'You can eat from any tree except the tree of the knowledge of good and evil. If you eat from that tree, you will surely die.'"

Miriam's voice, soft and kind, picked up the story. "The human was lonely, you know, being the only creature in the garden, so the LORD God created all kinds of animals and birds and brought them to the human like a parade, to name each one and see if any of them would be a suitable partner. But no luck."

"So," Miriam shrugged, "the LORD God made the human fall into a deep sleep and used one side to create a woman. When the man woke up, he was happy to have a partner."

""For a while, everything was perfect," Miriam continued. "The LORD God prepared a beautiful land for those first ancestors and allowed them to live there as long as they obeyed the LORD God's commands."

Samuel leaned in, "But one of the animals the LORD God created was trickier than the others. The human had named it 'snake.'"

We gasped. We knew about snakes. The slithering. The hissing. The striking!

"The snake asked the woman," here Samuel whispered in a sneaky tone, "'Did God really say you can't eat from any tree in the garden? That seems a bit strict, doesn't it?'"

We looked at each other curiously. We had never heard a snake talk! Samuel grinned and spoke excitedly, "The woman replied, 'We can eat from any tree except the one in the middle. If we even touch it, we will die.' But the snake scoffed, 'You won't die. If you eat the fruit, you'll become like God, knowing good and evil.'"

Miriam smiled at Samuel as she picked up the story, "The woman looked over at the fruit and thought, 'Maybe it will make me wise.' So she took a bite. She gave it to the man and he took a bite, too. As soon as they ate it, they realized they had been naked the whole time. Confused and embarrassed, they quickly sewed leaves together to make clothes."

We laughed as we imagined the scene and the leafy clothes. "You might laugh now but they were scared." Samuel's voice was firm. "At that moment, they heard the LORD God walking in the garden. They ran and hid among the trees. 'Where are you?' called the LORD God. The man answered, 'I was afraid because I was naked, so I hid.' The LORD God asked, 'Who told you that you were naked? Did you eat from the tree I told you not to eat from?'

The man responded, 'The woman—you know, the one you gave me?— she gave me some fruit and I ate it.' So the LORD God turned to the woman, 'What have you done?' And the woman responded, 'The snake—you know, the one you made?—it tricked me and I ate it.' The LORD God cursed the snake, the woman, and the ground because of the man. Then the LORD made proper clothes for the humans and said, 'Now they are like us—they know good and evil. We must send them away so they cannot eat from the tree of life and live forever.'"

Everyone was quiet as Samuel finished the story, "So the LORD God exiled our ancestors from the garden and placed angels and a flaming sword to guard the tree of life."

Miriam's voice was gentle as she spoke. "We have followed in the footsteps of our first ancestors. The LORD God prepared a beautiful land for us and put us there to tend to it. We were told that we could stay in the land as long as we obeyed the LORD God's commandments. But we did not. And we too have been exiled to the east."

We lowered our heads, hearts heavy with sadness for the home we left behind. "But just like our ancestors," Miriam said, "our story isn't over yet. We will trust. And have hope."

Teaching

The first five books in the Bible—Genesis, Exodus, Leviticus, Numbers, and Deuteronomy—are sometimes known as the Pentateuch, which is a Greek word that means "five scrolls."

Jewish people call these first five books the Torah, which is a Hebrew word that means "to teach." (Hebrew is the language the Torah was written in. It was later translated into Greek, which is why we also have the Greek name Pentateuch.)

Within the Torah we find laws, stories, songs, poems, lists of people in families, myths, and many other ancient ways of storytelling. All of these genres—these ways of storytelling— are needed to "teach" people.

The texts in the Torah, like the rest of the Bible, were written by many people in many places over a long period of time. But it was after the Babylonian exile that these five books were organized and arranged into something resembling the Torah as we know it today.

This is why many of these stories seem concerned with questions from that time: questions about who the people of God are, why bad things happen, and where God is when they do.

As you read through these stories, think about which questions they might be answering. Can you "hear" some of the conversations among these texts?

The one where God creates...again

IN OUR IMAGE

As told by Mari Jørstad

———————

At first God created the sky and the land.
The land was a big mess.
Above the mess it was dark.
God's wind flew over the water.
God said:
"I want light."
The light came on!
God looked at the light.
God liked it.
God split the light from the dark.
God gave the name "day" to the light.
To the dark, God gave the name "night."
It was evening. It was morning. The first day.

* * * * * * * * *

God said:
"I want a ceiling to cut through the water.
I want it to split the water in two."
God made the ceiling.
It split the water under the ceiling
from the water over the ceiling.
Look: it's all done.
God gave the name "sky" to the ceiling.
It was evening. It was morning. The second day.

****

God said:
"I want the waters under the sky
to get together.
I want dry places to pop up."
Look: it's all done.
God gave the name "land" to the dry places.
To the waters, God gave the name "sea."
God looked at the land and the sea.
God liked them.
God said:
"I want the land to grow green things:
Plants that sow seeds.
All kinds of fruit trees that make
fruit with seeds inside."
The land shot up green things:
Every plant that sows seeds,
Every tree that makes fruit with seeds inside.
God looked at the green things.
God liked them.
It was evening. It was morning. The third day.

****

God said:
"I want lights to sit in the sky ceiling, to split the day from the night.
I want the lights to tell everyone about celebrations and days and years.
I want the lights to shine on the land."
God made the two big lights:
The bigger light to rule the day,
The smaller light to rule the night,
And the stars.
God put them on the sky ceiling to shine on the land,
To rule the day and the night,

To split the light from the dark.
God looked at the lights.
God liked them.
It was evening. It was morning. The fourth day.

****

God said: "I want the waters to swarm with living, breathing,
swimming things.
I want birds to fly above the land and across the sky ceiling."
God created the big beasts,
Every living, breathing thing that crawls,
Everything that swarms in the waters, every winged bird.
God looked at the animals.
God liked them.
God blessed them:
"Bear fruit, have lots of babies, and fill the waters in the sea.
I want lots of birds."
It was evening. It was morning. The fifth day.

****

God said:
"I want the land to shoot up every kind
of living, breathing thing.
Farm animals and crawling animals
and wild animals,
Of every kind."
Look: it's all done.
God made every wild animal,
Every farm animal,
Every animal that crawls in the dirt.
God looked at the animals.
God liked them.

God said:
"We want to make people using
our shape and our image.
We want them to take care of the sea fish, The sky birds, the farm
animals,
The whole land,
All the crawling things that crawl on the land."
God made people using God's shape,
Using God's shape, God made people.
God made man and woman.
God blessed them and said to them:
"Bear fruit, have lots of babies,
fill the land, and make paths.
Take care of the fish in the sea,
The birds in the sky,
All living, crawling things in the land."
God said: "Listen up!
I give you every plant sowing seeds
that is in the land,
Every tree that makes fruit with seeds inside.
They will be your food."
Every green plant is food
For all the wild animals in the land, all the birds of the sky,
All the crawling things in the land that have living breath.
Look: it's all done.
God looked at everything God had made.
Listen up! God liked it a lot!
It was evening. It was morning. The sixth day.

****

The sky and the land and all the families living there were done.
On the seventh day, God was done with God's work.
God rested on the seventh day from all the work

God had been working on.
God blessed the seventh day and made it holy,
Because on that day God rested from all God's work,
Which God created for God to do.

Creation Stories

The Bible begins with two different stories of creation: this poem, and the story in the Garden of Eden. These were probably written at different times in different places for different people, but both were important to the Bible's ancient storytellers and both tell us something about how ancient people understood God, people, and the world around them.

People in ancient times thought the earth was flat, not round. They thought the land sat above a large, underground sea. They thought the sky was a hard ceiling and that the sun, moon, and stars were stuck to it. They thought there was more water above this ceiling.

The Bible's storytellers and their neighbors all thought this was the shape of the world. When they wrote about how God made the world, they used this picture of the universe. This might seem strange to us, but the really strange thing about this creation poem—told in Genesis chapter 1—is what it says about people.

Genesis 1 says God makes people using God's shape and image.

Many ancient creation myths said the gods made people because they were tired of work and they wanted someone else (people!) to do it. But in Genesis 1, God works. People, animals, and trees are not created to work for God, though they do receive responsibilities. And God blesses the people with a day of rest—the sabbath. A day to rest and worship God.

The one with the do-over

RE-CREATION

As told by Jonathan Lewis-Jong

'Twas a dark and stormy night…then another, and another. For forty days and forty nights God sent rain and more rain, till all the Earth was covered, even the tips and tops of the tallest mountains.

The world looked empty, like before creation. There was only deep, dark water as far as the eye could see.

Not that there were many eyes left to see it: the land animals had drowned, and so had the winged creatures who once flew across the vault of the sky.

All of the humans were dead, too. Well, not all of the humans. There was still Noah and his family, but we'll get to them soon.

First, the flood. The flood that reversed all of the good work God did in creation. Why would God send a flood at all?

Perhaps because heavenly beings—like angels, maybe—were mingling with human women, who then gave birth to giants. God did not approve of that. Or maybe it was because people were fighting all the time with one another—that they were very naughty, even in their hearts. God did not approve of that either. The Bible's storytellers give us two different reasons and both are difficult to understand.

In any case, everyone agreed that God looked at the world and saw that it was not very good after all. Well, not good except for Noah.

Because it turns out the world was not totally empty. On the surface of the deep floated a wooden boat. In the boat was a man named Noah. And with Noah were his sons: Shem, Ham, and Japheth. Noah's wife was with him too, but we do not know her name. Noah's sons' wives were also in the boat, but we do not know their names either. (You might notice an awkward pattern here.)

And on board the ark with Noah and his family were a bunch of animals. After all, it was not the animals' fault the humans were so awful that God wanted to begin again.

You see, before the rains fell, God told Noah to fetch these animals: one pair of every kind, one male and one female—or perhaps it was seven pairs of some kinds and one pair of others (more of the ones that were acceptable for eating, you understand). Our storytellers left two sets of instructions here, too.

Either way, they would need a very big boat. So God told Noah to build an ark three hundred cubits long. A cubit was an ancient way of measuring length, like a yard or a metre. So Noah built this very big boat, but it was not quite as big as the Titanic.

Into the boat they went, Noah and his family and all the animals, and there they waited. Seven days they waited; and then the rain began and it did not stop until the tips and tops of mountains were covered.

And so it was for one hundred and fifty days: an empty world, but for the boat on the surface of the deep.

Eventually, the waters began to subside, and the boat no longer floated along, but came to rest. Atop a mountain, it rested, and there it remained for forty days. In it Noah remained too, with his family and all the animals.

At the end of forty days, Noah opened a window and released a raven. Nobody knows what happened to the raven, but it did not return. (Some say it found meat to eat, floating on the water. What meat, I will leave to your imagination.)

So Noah sent a dove, which did return, finding neither foothold nor food, as doves are (mostly) vegetarians. And so Noah knew that the waters had not yet subsided. Seven days later, he tried again, and now the dove returned with an olive leaf. From this Noah knew that the waters had subsided at least to the treetops. Seven days later, he released the dove for a third time. When it did not return, Noah knew that it had found dry ground.

Out then they came, Noah and his family, and the animals: the livestock and wild animals, those that crawled and those that flew. Then Noah took some of the animals, whom he had saved from the flood, and sacrificed them to God in a fire, which is a bit ironic.

Then God promised Noah and all living creatures that such a disaster would never again befall the Earth. As a sign of this, God made a rainbow, which forms when light passes through droplets of water just so, exiting at various angles: but for more information about that, you will need to consult a science book, which this is not.

The end.

...Well, there is another bit of the story, but we will leave that for another day.

God Did What?!

Stories can help us understand the world around us. They help us understand who we are and why the world is the way it is.

Science does this, too. It can help us understand who we are and why the world is the way it is.

Ancient storytellers were not scientists, at least not as we understand "science" today. Today, when there is a big weather event, scientists can gather all kinds of data (like air temperatures and wind currents) that help explain why a flood, storm, or drought happened.

Ancient people didn't have these tools. When floods, droughts, or really anything at all happened, they thought they happened because God (or the gods) wanted them to happen.

There were lots of stories about floods and storms in the ancient world, and often these floods resulted in new creation. One story said the gods flooded the world because there were too many people making much too much noise! (Not the best of reasons, but relatable.) Ancient Canaanites thought the storm god Ba'al sent the rains and floods.

Ancient stories, like the stories of Noah, helped ancient people make sense of their world. Though they might not give us scientific answers for why things happened, they can tell us a lot about how ancient people understood God and the world around them.

A WANDERING ARAMEAN

As told by Lauren O'Connell

And this is the line of Terah: Terah begot Abram, Nahor, and Haran, and
Haran begot Lot...which is just an old-fashioned way of saying these were
Terah's children and this was Abram's family. There's an awful lot of "begetting"
in the Bible, but not, it seemed, for Abram.

Abram and his wife, Sarai, had been married for many years. Each morning
they woke up in their father's home. Each day they worked alongside their
brother and nephew. And each night, they fell asleep under the big starry skies
of Babylonia. Day after day, season after season, year after year.

As the years wore on, Abram's beard turned grey and the smiley crinkles
around Sarai's eyes turned into wrinkles. Abram and Sarai were growing old,
and although growing old is a gift (especially in the ancient world!), Sarai's
heart was sad. Every crinkle-turned-wrinkle reminded her of the baby she
did not have and might never have. There had been no begetting of sons or
daughters for Abram. And this broke Sarai's heart.

Because Sarai longed for a baby.

She longed for a child she could count the stars with. Laugh with. Talk
with and work with. A child she could tell stories to. Whose eyes crinkled
when they smiled. She longed for a baby so much that her whole body ached
from it. But year after year, no child came.

When so many years had passed that the idea of Abram begetting anyone
had begun to seem silly, the family left their home in Babylonia to begin a
new life in the land of Canaan. But sadness is a tricky thing and longing is
a very good traveler: Sarai's sadness and her longing traveled with her to her
new home in Haran.

Now Haran is not quite Canaan, but it was here that the family settled. Eventually, their dad Terah died and Abram became the patriarch of a family with no babies. (Patriarch is an old-fashioned way of saying "the man who is the boss of the family." The Bible has lots of old-fashioned ideas like this because the Bible is very old.)

One day, Abram the patriarch was minding his own business when the Lord called out to him, "Go from your land and your birthplace and your father's house to the land I will show you. And I will make you a great nation and I will bless you and make your name great, and through you all of the families on earth will be blessed." Now this was a bit weird because Abram had already left his birthplace and his dad had already died, but we're going to roll with it because Abram did.

So Abram and his nephew Lot gathered their goats and their tents and just about everything they could carry, and Sarai packed up their clothes and their blankets and bundled them up with her sadness, and the family set off for the land of Canaan...again.

I know what you're thinking: it must have been a bit of a surprise, having to pack up and move all over again. Well, just you wait, because the real surprise is coming!

When they arrived in the land of Canaan, the Lord appeared to Abram and said, "To your children, I will give this land."

Well this was awkward...

Maybe God didn't know that Abram had no children? Maybe God didn't know that Sarai's crinkles had turned into wrinkles? Maybe God didn't know that the chances of Abram and Sarai begetting a baby now that they were well and truly old were slim to none?!

God did know, actually. But Abram was confused! "Um, Lord," he said, "You haven't given me any children."

And the Lord said, "Abram, you will have children. Look to the heavens and count the stars—that's how many children, grandchildren and great-grandchildren you will have."

Abram believed the Lord.

As the sun set, Abram fell into a deep sleep. In the terrible darkness the Lord told Abram that his children would one day live as strangers in a strange land. That they would be enslaved and oppressed, but even then, there would be hope.

"To your children," the LORD whispered, "I will give this land, from the river of Egypt to the great River Euphrates."

But to Sarai, whose heart ached for a baby, no promises were made. Well, not yet anyway. So Sarai began making a plan of her own…

You Said That Already!

God makes lots of promises to Abram and although they sound sort of the same, each one is different.

For example, God promises Abram's children the land of Canaan, which is what the lands later known as the kingdoms of Israel and Judah used to be called. Later God promises Abram's children "all of the land between the river of Egypt and the great River Euphrates," which is much bigger than Canaan. In fact, it looks a lot like the lands the people spread throughout after the exile.

Abram and Sarai's story has lots of repeated bits, too, as well as bits that seem to be in the wrong order, like when God tells Abram to leave his birthplace and his father's house after those things had already happened.

Wait…does the Bible have mistakes?!

Nope. These repeated bits and stories with different details are some of the ways we can "hear" the voices of the different storytellers in the Bible. Like with Noah and the different reasons given for the flood. The people gathering these stories kept each of these voices—even when they disagreed or did not match.

These are not mistakes—preserving these voices and traditions is what the Bible was designed to do! And it's one of the best things about it. Many voices are needed to tell God's stories—including yours!

The one with the God who sees

HEY THERE, STRANGER

As told by Carolyn Custis James

Hagar's story is a story about an outsider—someone who was not the center of attention and who did not belong. Have you ever felt like that? Many of us do, at times.

Hagar was Egyptian. She was young, enslaved, foreign (to her storytellers), and female. Her name even means "the stranger" in Hebrew! But that's not how God saw Hagar. Her story reminds us that no one is a stranger to God.

****

Hagar was enslaved by Sarai. This means Hagar was part of Abram and Sarai's household, but she had to work for them and do whatever they said, and she could not leave, even if they treated her badly. And they did treat her badly— very badly. Neither Sarai nor Abram thought Hagar was important. They didn't even speak to her by name.

Already we can't help feeling something has gone horribly wrong in this story. But things are about to get even worse.

Remember how Sarai had a plan? Well that plan involved Hagar.

In the ancient world, a wealthy woman who did not have babies (like Sarai) was allowed to give a female she enslaved (like Hagar) to her husband to be an extra wife. If the enslaved girl gave birth to a son, the first wife could claim the son as her own.

That was Sarai's plan.

Of course, no one discussed this plan with Hagar. She was enslaved, so she had no choice. Hagar became Abram's wife. Then Hagar became pregnant.

Suddenly Hagar was important. Her belly got bigger and bigger as the baby grew inside her. For the first time, she held her head up high…and this made Sarai furious.

Sarai persuaded Abram to let her to punish Hagar. "Do what you want," Abram said. So Sarai severely mistreated Hagar.

Hagar fled into the wilderness where she collapsed in tears. That's when Hagar heard a voice. And for the first time in the story, Hagar was called by name.

"Hagar, slave-girl of Sarai! Where have you come from and where are you going?" The Angel of the Lord called out to her. God was searching for Hagar. She may have been a powerless outsider to Abram and Sarai, but Hagar was no outsider to God.

The Lord told Hagar, "Go back to Sarai and submit to her." That was a hard pill to swallow. But just as Sarai had a plan for Hagar, God had a plan, too:

> "Your child will be a boy and you will call him Ishmael.
> (Which means 'God hears.') He will be a wild man, fierce and independent."

"You are El Roi," Hagar said, "the God who Sees."

Hagar returned to Abram and Sarai, and bore her son—Ishmael. A son who would not be enslaved, but would grow up fierce and independent. But Hagar and Ishmael remained outsiders in Abram and Sarai's family.

During that time, God changed Abram's name to Abraham ("the father of many") and Sarai's name to Sarah ("princess"). But Hagar remained Hagar, the mother of Ishmael.

When Sarah was 90 years old she finally gave birth to a son. Abraham and Sarah named him Isaac, which means "laughter," for he brought the elderly couple great joy. But that joy was not shared with Hagar and Ishmael. Now that Sarah had a baby, she was determined that Isaac would be Abraham's only heir. She insisted that Abraham send Hagar and Ishmael away.

Reluctantly, Abraham did. He sent them into the desert of Beersheba with only a small amount of food and water. Both quickly ran out. Without food and water, Hagar and Ishmael would not survive. Hagar couldn't bear to watch her son die. Amid her tears, Hagar again heard the Angel of the LORD:

"Do not be afraid; God has heard the boy crying as he lies there.
Lift the boy up and take him by the hand, for I will make him into
a great nation."

Hagar opened her eyes and saw a well full of water. She and Ishmael were saved.

God had not forgotten Hagar or Ishmael—they were not strangers or outsiders
to El Roi. The Bible's storytellers remembered Hagar and Ishmael, too. They
remembered their stories and retold them over and over. Hagar and Ishmael
mattered to God, and you do, too.

Reading Well

One of the things you might notice as you read through the stories in the Bible is that things happen in them that are not okay. In fact, they are downright wrong.

Two of these things happen in this story. First, Hagar is enslaved by Sarai and Abram. And second, they use her body without her consent to grow their family. (Consent is when we agree to something freely, without fear of being hurt or punished.)

These things are 100% wrong. It is never okay for one person to enslave another or for one person to use another person's body without their consent. Ever.

But here is the weird thing: the Bible doesn't actually say this. It would be nice if it did, but it doesn't, and that is because the Bible's stories reflect the world in which their storytellers lived.

So we must read these hard stories well. We must read them alongside stories like Genesis 1, which says God made every single person in God's own image. And alongside the prophets, who remind us that God loves justice and hates oppression (when someone uses their power or position to treat others cruelly or unfairly).

We must read these hard stories in conversation with the other texts in the Bible and in conversation with God. Then ask ourselves, "Does this sound like God's plan for us? Or are these terrible things a reflection of the storytellers' world?"

The one with Rebekah and Isaac

A FAMILY AFFAIR

As told by Sarah Shectman

———————

One day, an Aramean girl named Rebekah went to the local well to get water for her family, just like she did every afternoon. But this day, something was a little different: there was a stranger at the well. With camels. Camels carrying gifts and supplies for a long trip across the desert.

This was suprising, not just because strangers didn't turn up at the well all that often, but because camels didn't help people in this way for at least another few hundred years. They were still pretty wild in Rebekah's time, so it's kind of wild that they are in this story!

Nevertheless, Rebekah took the stranger—and the camels—in her stride. The stranger asked Rebekah to share some of her water with him. Her parents had taught her that it was important to be kind to travelers, so she gave him some, and she also got water for his camels. That was a lot of water, since camels can drink a lot, especially after a long trip across the desert.

"Tell me, whose daughter are you?" the man asked Rebekah.

"My father is Bethuel, the son of Nahor and Milcah," she answered.

The stranger was astonished. You see, Rebekah was just the person he had come looking for.

The stranger was the servant of Abraham, and Nahor was Abraham's brother. Abraham's son Isaac—the baby Sarah had waited for and wanted for so long—was all grown up and old enough to get married. But Abraham really wanted Isaac to marry a woman from his own people just like he had, so he sent his servant back to his home country to find a wife for Isaac from his own clan. The servant had agreed to go find a wife for Isaac, but during his long trek across the desert, he'd had plenty of time to worry about all the things that could go wrong.

What if he couldn't find Abraham's clan? What if he found the clan but they didn't have any unmarried daughters? What if he found the clan and they had an unmarried daughter, but she wouldn't agree to trek all the way back over the desert to marry someone she'd never even seen? I mean, why would she?! It all seemed kind of...unrealistic.

But Abraham had been very clear: no way was Isaac going back to Aram to get married. Abraham didn't want Isaac to leave the land God had promised, not even to go find a wife. So the servant went for him.

Abraham had told the servant to have faith that God would make his mission a success. Luckily, Abraham was right. Here was a woman from Abraham's own family, drawing water from the well for him and his camels to drink!

So the servant spoke with Rebekah's father Bethuel and her brother Laban and told them of Abraham's son, Isaac, and of his long journey to Aram, and of meeting Rebekah at the well. Bethuel and Laban agreed that it did sound like God had organized things wonderfully. They spoke with Rebekah, and she agreed to go back to Canaan with the servant and marry Isaac. She got on one of the camels and rode with the servant back across the desert.

When they finally arrived, dusty and tired, and she saw Isaac, she fell off her camel. Isaac took Rebekah to his mother Sarah's tent—the part of Abraham's encampment where he lived—and they were married.

But just like Sarah before her, Rebekah had trouble having a baby. She waited and waited, and Isaac prayed and prayed. Who would inherit the blessing and the promises God made to Abraham? Who would become a great nation and fill the land with children and grandchildren and great-grandchildren if Rebekah couldn't have a baby?

Finally Rebekah fell pregnant. But her pregnancy was difficult—her belly roiled and rumbled. So she went to ask an oracle (a person who says they can communicate directly with God) why this was happening to her. The oracle told Rebekah she was having twin boys—that there were not one but two babies in her belly. "Two nations," the LORD said, "and two peoples— one people will be stronger than the other, and the older will serve the younger."

Now Isaac would have not one but two sons!

Inheritances

You may have noticed by now that when it comes right down to it, the stories we have been reading—which are found in the book of Genesis—are stories about family. And this family—Abraham and Sarah's family—has a lot of the same experiences that families today have. They want to have babies and sometimes have trouble getting pregnant.

Their children don't always get along. Someone gets jealous of someone else. They worry about who their kids are going to marry. You know the drill. But this family has another thing to worry about and fight over: Who would inherit the promises of land and the covenants that God made with Abraham?

Usually it was the oldest son who inherited the family land in ancient Israel, but in Genesis, it is not. In these stories, the younger sons inherit the promises of the land. Although Hagar's son Ishmael receives a special blessing from God and becomes a "great nation," it is Abraham's younger son Isaac, his son by Sarah, who inherits the promises of land. And so it is with Isaac's sons, too.

But these stories are much more than simple family tales. The sons in these stories represent nations—the storytellers and their neighbors—kingdoms and peoples of the ancient world. These family stories helped the storytellers understand the world around them, and their relationships with neighboring peoples and kingdoms.

The one where Jacob wrestles

ISRAEL, IS IT?

As told by Rachel Starr

Even before they were born, Rebekah's sons struggled to get along. Esau entered the world first, full of energy and covered in hair. Second came Jacob, grasping his brother's heel as they were born, not wanting to be left behind. Some say the twins divided their family, but maybe they balanced it out.

In those days, just like today, people went hungry. Esau was often hungry. Coming in from the fields one day, he smelt something delicious. Jacob had been cooking. And Esau? Could. Not. Wait.

"Give me some of that red stew," he said to his brother. But Jacob refused until Esau had given him something he wanted—Esau's birthright.

Their father Isaac was often hungry, too. One day, he asked Esau to bring him his favorite meal and promised to bless him on his return. But Rebekah overheard and, while Esau was out hunting, she told Jacob to put on his brother's coat and rough animal skins. Then she gave Jacob his father's favorite meal to take to him. (Parents don't often have favorite children, but Rebekah did and hers was Jacob. Isaac's was Esau.) When Isaac, who was blind, placed his hands on Jacob, he believed the smooth talking trickster was his hairy son Esau and blessed him.

When Rebekah and Jacob's trick was discovered, everyone was angry! As the firstborn son, that blessing belonged to Esau, and Jacob had all but stolen it. So Jacob was sent away.

Many years later and far from home, it was Jacob's turn to be tricked. His uncle had two daughters called Leah and Rachel. For seven long years, Jacob worked for the chance to marry Rachel, only to discover that he had been tricked into marrying her sister Leah! Seven more years he worked and at last he and Rachel were together. But Jacob's love could not make Rachel happy because she longed for children and did not have any.

The two sister-wives struggled and schemed: Rachel for children, and Leah for love. And just like Jacob's grandma Sarah, they involved two women they enslaved, Bilhah and Zilpah, never asking them what they wanted.

At last, Rachel gave birth to a child and Jacob felt his family was complete. He was ready to return home. Before he left, he tricked his uncle into giving him the best and strongest sheep and goats. Then, he took Leah and Rachel, Bilhah and Zilpah, children and animals—and ran!

Now Jacob felt ready to meet Esau again. Perhaps he was finally sorry for tricking him. Or perhaps he felt strong in his success. Or perhaps he just missed his brother.

But even though he sought out Esau, Jacob was soon back to his old tricks. He divided up his flock and family to hide them from Esau. He asked God for protection from his brother. And he sent Esau gifts to smooth the way ahead. Preparations made, he and his family rested for the night.

But in the darkness, Jacob woke with a start. Would Esau still be angry with him? Jacob could not shake off his fears. So he sent Leah and Rachel, Bilhah and Zilpah, his eleven sons and one daughter across the River Jabbok, past the guardian of the ford, who had been there for as long as anyone could remember.

Jacob was alone. But not for long.

A stranger came and wrestled with him, just as he had wrestled in the womb with his brother. All through the night, Jacob and the stranger held each other close. As the day began to break, the stranger struck Jacob's hip and he cried out with pain. But he didn't let go. "Not until I know your name, not until you bless me," Jacob said.

"Tell me your name and I will bless you," the stranger replied. So Jacob told the stranger who he was—no tricks this time. And the stranger blessed him with a new name: "Israel," the one who wrestled in fear and faith.

Even though it was still too dark to see the stranger's face, Jacob let go. He wondered if he had wrestled all night with the river guardian, an angel, or even God.

But the face he longed to see most of all was that of his brother Esau. A new day began as Jacob-now-Israel limped away toward his brother, rivals no more.

Esau had many children, as did Israel. These were the sons of Israel, born of love and sorrow, chosen and unchosen: born to Leah were Reuben, Simeon, Levi, Judah, Issachar, and Zebulun, and daughter Dinah. To Zilpah, Gad and Asher. To Bilhah, Dan and Naphtali. And to Rachel, Joseph and Benjamin, last but not least.

Imagine

Close your eyes and imagine Jacob wrestling the stranger. What do you see?

Maybe the picture in your mind looks like the picture of Jacob and Esau wrestling at the beginning of this story? This makes sense, because the pictures we see in real life help our minds understand stories.

The story of Jacob wrestling with the stranger has been painted and portrayed by many artists in many different ways over the centuries. But how they picture the story—their perspective—can be very different. How might seeing this story from another perspective change how we understand the story?

Some artists place us in the middle, caught between Jacob and the stranger.

We feel muscles strain and hear gasps for breath. There is no space between them!

Other artists help us see things from a distance: the other side of the river, perhaps, standing with Leah and Rachel, Bilhah and Zilpah, and all their children. We can't quite make out what is happening, who has the upper hand, and we wonder how it will turn out.

Every painting or sculpture helps us see the stories of the Bible in new ways. They remind us that the same story can look different to each of us.

As you read through this book and look at its pictures, imagine—what might it look like to see things from a different perspective?

HERE COMES THE DREAMER

As told by Safwat Marzouk

Joseph was the second-youngest child in a very big family. His father, Jacob (also known as Israel), had twelve sons, as well as daughters, and Joseph was the dreamer. He had dreams of becoming a great person.

Maybe this was because Joseph knew he had a special place in his father's heart. Joseph was born to Jacob in his old age, the son of Jacob's favorite wife, Rachel, who died giving birth to Joseph's little brother. Jacob took extra special care of Joseph, but perhaps Jacob was mistaken to favor Joseph over his brothers.

One day, Jacob gave Joseph a very special robe. His brothers saw that their father loved Joseph more than any other and they became jealous of him. They hated Joseph even more when he told them about his dreams. To be fair, Joseph probably sounded arrogant when he revealed them: In his dreams all of his brothers bowed down to him!

But none of this excuses the horror of what his brothers did next. They treated Joseph like a piece of property by selling him to some passing Ishmaelites (Ishmael's descendants), who then sold Joseph as a slave to an Egyptian man named Potiphar.

Enslaved in Egypt, Joseph was miles away from his family and very far from his dreams of greatness. We do not know how Joseph felt at this point—Was he sad? Lonely? Hurt? Resentful? What we do know is that he did not give up.

Working among strangers in the house of Potiphar, Joseph was diligent and faithful in doing all of the tasks given to him. Soon enough, because of his honesty and his hard work, Joseph became a supervisor in Potiphar's house and things began to feel like they would work out.

But one day all of this was shattered.

Potiphar's wife had always liked Joseph, but perhaps she liked him a little too much. One day, when Potiphar was out of the house, his wife tried to get Joseph to betray Potiphar. But Joseph would not do anything that would displease God, so he ran from Potiphar's wife. Angry, Potiphar's wife told a big lie: She accused Joseph of doing the very thing he refused to do! Even though Potiphar liked Joseph, he did not listen to Joseph's side of the story. Maybe because Joseph was a slave from a faraway land, who did not have much power. And so, Joseph was thrown into prison.

Joseph was like many migrants who live away from their homeland—even though he was not treated fairly by the people in this new land, he did not give up. Joseph did what he did best, even in prison: he worked hard, he was honest, and he treated others kindly.

It was while he was in prison that Joseph the dreamer began interpreting other people's dreams. Pharaoh's baker and cup bearer had dreams that they did not understand until Joseph explained what they meant.

Two years passed while Joseph waited in prison. Then one night Pharaoh, the king of Egypt, had two dreams—or rather nightmares. He saw seven strong cows eaten by seven weak cows, and seven strong ears of grain swallowed by seven weak ears of grain. Pharaoh was terrified. None of his wise advisors could explain what his dreams meant.

Everyone in the palace was anxious until Pharaoh's cup bearer remembered Joseph, who had interpreted his dreams when he was in prison. They rushed to get Joseph.

When Pharaoh told Joseph about his dreams, Joseph knew that God had shown Pharaoh what was about happen. He explained that the strong cows and ears of grain were years in which there would be plenty of food in Egypt. But this would be followed by seven years of severe famine, when no one would have enough to eat.

Joseph suggested the Egyptians should store the extra food during the years of plenty so that they would have enough to eat during the famine. Pharaoh was so impressed with Joseph's wisdom that he told people Joseph had the spirit of God in him. Then he put Joseph in charge of collecting the extra food and storing it, ready for the famine.

The famine came and Joseph's brothers were forced to travel to Egypt to buy food. There they found themselves bowing down to a powerful man they did not recognize. The powerful man was Joseph! Just like in Joseph's dream from long ago. When Joseph revealed himself to them, they were terrified. They thought Joseph would take revenge on them for the terrible thing they had done when they sold him to the Ishmaelites. But Joseph forgave his brothers, who were really very sorry they had been so awful. They all wept as they hugged and were reconciled.

Joseph's brothers settled in Egypt with Joseph and raised their families there. And Joseph realized that his dreams and the power he had were given to him so that he could save his family and the Egyptians from the famine.

On the Move

Joseph was enslaved and he was also a forced migrant—someone who is forced to leave their homeland and live in a foreign land.

This sounds a lot like what happened to those who were exiled from their homeland by the Babylonian soldiers, doesn't it? It also sounds a lot like the stories of many people today and throughout history who have had to leave their homes because of war, violence, climate change, famine, or poverty.

Even though Joseph experienced trauma at the hands of his family, and in Egypt at the hands of Potiphar and his wife, he did not give up. He was able to overcome these very hard things and use his wisdom to save his family and the Egyptians from famine.

Joseph's story helped those living far from home after the Babylonian exile to believe that not only could they survive outside the lands they were born in, but they also could thrive and be a blessing to the nations around them.

Joseph's story presents Egypt as a place of refuge for migrants. After the exile, many people from Judah (Judeans) lived in Egypt and made lives for themselves there, just like Joseph. They even built a temple there!

Joseph's story reminded those in positions of power to offer hospitality to migrants in place of injustice and oppression.

The one with Moses

HERE I AM

As told by Chauncey Diego Francisco Handy

God's friend Moses grew up in Egypt. Moses's people, the Hebrews, had lived in Egypt for 400 years—ever since their ancestors, the children of Israel, had left Canaan to settle in Egypt with the brother they had sold into slavery. But now the new Pharaoh was scared. He worried that the Hebrews would try to take over his kingdom. There were so many of them, after all. "We have to keep them in line, otherwise they'll help our enemies!" he said.

Pharaoh enslaved all of the Hebrew people and ordered two Hebrew midwives, Puah and Shiphrah, to kill the baby boys as they were born. But these midwives knew their job was to help mothers birth life into the world, not to deliver death. They bravely defied Pharaoh.

But Pharaoh was determined. So he ordered the Egyptian people to throw any Hebrew baby boy they found into the Nile River.

When Moses was born, his mother hid her beautiful baby boy until he was too big to keep secret. With a broken heart, she put Moses in a waterproof basket and set him among the reeds on the River Nile. His sister waited and kept watch over the basket.

Soon, a princess (a daughter of Pharaoh) came to the river to take a bath and saw Moses crying in the basket. "This is one of the Hebrew babies," she said to herself. Then and there she decided to raise him, even though she knew her father's law about Hebrew baby boys.

"Do you need someone to nurse the baby?" asked Moses's sister.

"Why, yes I do!" said the princess.

Moses's sister helped the Egyptian princess find someone to nurse Moses—his mother!

When he was old enough, Moses's mother brought Moses to Pharaoh's daughter to be raised as her son. Though Moses grew up as the grandson of Pharaoh, he knew he was a Hebrew and he saw the way the Hebrews were enslaved and mistreated. It made him so angry that one day he killed an Egyptian who was hurting a Hebrew. When Pharaoh heard this, he sent soldiers to find Moses—so Moses ran. He ran all the way to the land of Midian.

When Moses got to Midian, he sat down next to a well. Just then the seven daughters of Jethro, the priest of Midian, came to get their sheep some water. Moses helped the girls water their flock, and when the girls got home, they told their father, Reuel, what had happened. (Did you notice their dad's name just changed? This is one of those times our storytellers tell the same story with different details. It happens a lot in Exodus.)

"An Egyptian helped us!" the girls said.

"What? Why did you leave him there?! Invite him to dinner!" their father said.

At dinner, their father invited Moses to stay with him. Moses stayed and he got very close to the family—he even married one of the daughters, Zipporah!

One day, Moses was minding sheep on Mount Horeb, when he saw a bush on fire—but it wasn't burning up. "I've gotta see this. Why isn't that bush burning up?!" Moses thought.

When the LORD saw that Moses was looking at the bush, God called to him, "Moses, Moses!"

"Here I am!" Moses answered. (This is the way God's friends answer God—even if they don't know they're God's friends yet).

"Take off your sandals, please. This is my special mountain!" God said. "I am the God of your father—the God of Abraham, the God of Isaac, and the God of Jacob."

Moses closed his eyes—he was afraid to look at God.

Then God said, "I have seen the suffering of my people—heard them crying out because of the Egyptians, their enslavers. So, I will deliver them from Egypt and will bring them up from Egypt to a good land—a land flowing with milk and honey. The home of the Canaanites, Hittites,

Amorites, Perizzites, Hivites, and Jebusites. And I will send YOU to Pharaoh to bring the Israelites out of Egypt."

"I don't think I'm the right person," Moses said.

"I will be with you the whole time," God replied. But Moses wasn't convinced.

"Okay, let's say I go to the Israelites and say 'The God of your ancestors sent me' and then they say 'What's the name of that God?' What am I supposed to say?" he asked.

"'I WILL BE WHO I WILL BE,'" God said. " Tell them I AM has sent you."

Moses still wasn't sure. But after *a lot* more convincing, Moses accepted God's plan and went to see Pharaoh.

What's in a Name?

Names are really important in the Bible. Take Moses, for example. When the princess names him she says, "Because I drew him out of the water." Mosheh, Moses's name in Hebrew, does sound like "mashah," a Hebrew word that means "to pull or draw out."

The names of the people are also important. Sometimes, they are called Hebrews. At other times, they are known as Israel, which is also the name given to Jacob and the name of a kingdom. Confusing!

But God's names are perhaps the most important of all. In this story, God reveals a very special name to Moses: YHWH, which means something like "I am who I am" or "I will be who I will be." This name is so special that many Jewish people will not say it. Instead they say "Adonai," which means "My Lord," or "HaShem," which means "the name." We don't ever write this special name in our Bibles! Wherever this name appears in the Hebrew text, we use "the LORD" in our English translations.

God has many names in the Bible. El Shaddai, El Roi, Elohim, YHWH, YHWH-Jireh, and lots, lots more! Some people who study the Bible think some storytellers use certain names for God more than others. Kind of like how one person might call their mother "Mom" and another might call them "Mum"—the different names for God might be clues to the different voices in the text.

35

The one with the exodus

BY THIS THEY WILL KNOW

As told by Brent A. Strawn

Things don't begin well with Pharaoh. Moses and his brother Aaron deliver the LORD's message to Pharaoh, just as the LORD told them to: "The LORD says, 'Let my people go!'"

But the Egyptian king is stern: "Nope. Won't do it. Also, who is this 'Lord' person you're talking about? Never heard of him."

Pharaoh's response is funny (and ironic) because we are never told Pharaoh's own name. "Pharaoh" is a title, the Egyptian word for "king." Egypt's pharaohs did have names, but our story doesn't care what Pharaoh's name is, because this story is not about this king—this story is about God. In fact, by refusing to provide a name for Pharaoh, the storytellers show us that what God does in this story is not about one specific ruler at one specific time in one specific place—it's about all rulers in all times and all places. But we're getting ahead of ourselves. Back to Moses and Aaron and Pharaoh…

Pharaoh is unimpressed with Moses and the LORD. He will need convincing. In the meantime, he makes things worse: the enslaved Hebrews are given no relief. Instead, their work is made harder and they are beaten for it. They complain to Pharaoh, but he doesn't care.

"You're unjust!" they say. "You're lazy!" he replies.

Then things get EVEN WORSE! Pharaoh's mistreatment crushes the Israelites' spirit, making them doubt Moses and Aaron. That makes Moses doubt God, his calling, and this whole mission.

When Moses complains to God, God promises to deliver the Israelites with a mighty hand and an outstretched arm. Now we might not know what that means, but Moses did, because ancient Egyptian artists used to paint pharaohs in this pose. This time it's God who strikes the pose. And "strike" is exactly the right word for what happens next.

First, God sends Moses and Aaron to Pharaoh with a message: "Let my people go!" To make sure Pharaoh pays attention, God turns Aaron's staff into a snake.

But Pharaoh does not listen. So God turns the water in the mighty Nile River to blood.

Still Pharaoh doesn't listen. So God sends a plague of frogs on all of Egypt. "Okay, this is really bad," says Pharaoh. "I'll let the people leave." But when God removes the frogs, Pharaoh changes his mind.

So God sends a plague of gnats, and then flies. "Okay, okay! You can go," says Pharaoh, only to change his mind...again!

Back and forth, plague after plague, it goes: Pharaoh says "Okay!" then changes his mind. The LORD even sends Egypt into darkness for three days! It takes ten awe-inspiring divine acts before Pharaoh finally lets Israel go. The Bible calls these acts "signs," perhaps because they point to something else, something really important—that God, not Pharaoh, is in control of Egypt. Through these signs God slowly un-creates Egypt, returning it to a chaotic state of darkness. Egypt is demolished and remade. In doing this, the people Israel, too, are remade. As the Hebrews watch God fight for them, they go from enslaved, overworked, sad people to God's treasured possession, who have a special relationship with the LORD.

But even after Pharaoh finally lets the people go, guess what happens next? Yes, Pharaoh changes his mind! AGAIN! He and his best troops chase the Hebrews until he has their back against the wall—or rather the sea; in this case, the Sea of Reeds.

Then comes God's most amazing act. Moses lifts up his staff and God splits the water in two, pushing back the waters with a divine wind, so Israel can pass through safely. Just like the first creation, God separates waters and brings forth dry land. Israel is re-created: no longer slaves to Pharaoh, they are now servants of the LORD. No wonder Moses, his sister Miriam, and all the Israelites with them burst into song:

I will sing to the LORD because the LORD has triumphed amazingly!
Horse and rider were thrown into the sea!
The LORD is my strength and my song!
The LORD is my deliverer!
This is my God. I will praise the LORD!
The LORD will rule forever and always!

The exodus from Egypt is remembered and retold throughout the Bible and ever since. Whenever people ask, "Who is God?," the stories of the exodus say, "The one who has power over all things, who loves God's people, and delivers them from oppression."

Bigger and Better

The ten signs are a bit scary. The storytellers clearly want to show that God is more powerful than Egypt and its many gods.

Right before God turns the Nile River to blood, God shows Pharaoh a miracle: Aaron's staff turns into a snake. When the Egyptian magicians do the same thing with their staffs, Aaron's staff eats theirs up! His is the best!

Before the tenth sign, God tells Moses, "I will judge all the Egyptian gods." The plagues show that the LORD, not the Egyptian gods, is in control of these events.

For example, Hapi is the Egyptian god of the Nile, but it is the LORD who turns the river to blood. And Re, the mightiest of the Egyptian gods—the god of the sun—is no match for the LORD, who puts Egypt in the dark.

Even Pharaoh, whose main job was to maintain order, an important idea related to an Egyptian goddess named Maat, is exposed as a fraud through the un-creation and chaos that takes place through the LORD's ten signs.

Each of these signs makes a statement: the LORD is bigger and better than all other gods and all human kings. By these acts—and the exodus from Egypt—everyone will learn and know who God is.

RULES TO LOVE BY

As told by Brent A. Strawn

On the other side of the Sea of Reeds lay the wilderness. Here the people wander and worry. Where will they find water to drink? What will they eat? Has the LORD freed them from Egypt just to abandon them in the wilderness?!

Of course not! God makes sure the people have everything they need. God draws water from a rock for drinking and sends the people manna (something like bread) from heaven every morning, exactly enough to fill their bellies so they can walk to the mountain that Moses is leading them to—the special mountain where they will worship God.

You see, worshipping God was the goal from the get-go.

Exactly three months after they escaped Pharaoh, the people reach God's mountain (which is sometimes called Sinai and sometimes called Horeb) and Moses goes up to meet God. Here is where the people enter into a very special relationship with God called a covenant—an unbreakable promise between two people or groups of people.

The first thing to say about this covenant between God and the people is that it represents a real relationship between them. Both are in this thing together. The second thing to say is that this covenant contains a lot of details: rules, regulations, and expectations for just about everything you could imagine...and then some! Altogether, these details are called *torah* and as we already know, *torah* in the Bible means much more than a simple listing of dos and don'ts. In the Bible, *torah* is a very big word, with lots of space in it!

Once Moses reaches the top of the mountain, God recaps what has happened so far: "You've seen everything I've done to the Egyptians, how I rescued you, and brought you here."

"Yes, we have," says Moses.

"Okay," says God, "So, now, if you want to be my treasured people for all time—even though *all people* and the *whole world* belongs to me—then you must listen to what I say and be obedient to this covenant we are making. Go back to the Israelites and tell them all this, then report back."

"Got it," says Moses, "Will do!"

So Moses does, and all of God's people say, "We will do everything the LORD says!"

Moses reports this back to God and the covenant is official. Now, Israel is God's people in more ways than one!

On top of the mountain, there is an amazing display of fireworks: thunder and lightning, cloud and thick smoke, fire, and a sound like the loudest trumpet—even an earthquake. It is almost like a volcano! But it is the LORD coming to the mountain to lay out the terms of the covenant. And there are a lot of terms!

The rules, regulations, and expectations that God has for Israel include everything from what they eat to how they dress to how they treat their parents, children, next-door neighbors, visitors, immigrants—even their enemies. The covenant contains rules about animals and sacrifices, farming and trees, business and shopping. Some have counted as many as 613 rules in God's law.

God's covenant begins in a special way—or, rather, two special ways. The very first rule reminds Israel who God is and what God has done for them: "I am your God, the LORD, who brought you out of Egypt—out of slavery!"

Everything that follows, all the laws and all the details, flow from this: God acted first, God saved, God delivered. God's people owe God everything in return: their very lives, which is huge, and also 613 specific ways to obey, which is a lot but pretty small in comparison.

The second special way the covenant begins is with a list of ten extremely important rules. They are so important that they are repeated twice in the Bible. Here they are:

> Be faithful to me and me only; do not worship anyone or anything else. Don't use my special name, "the LORD," in bad ways. (I really don't like that.) The seventh day of the week is special: I made it

for resting, not work. I rested on the seventh day of creation, plus you never got a day of rest in Egypt under Pharaoh. So be like me and don't be like Pharaoh. Treat your parents with respect. Don't kill. You who are married, keep your promises to love each other only. Don't steal. Don't tell lies about people. Don't desire things that aren't yours.

This sounds straightforward, doesn't it? But these rules can be hard for people to keep, even God's covenant people. That's sad, but it's also something that God expected. So, God's covenant includes ways to say sorry and set things right, with God and with others, whenever we fail to obey. That's another thing that makes God's law so great!

Covenants

Covenants were very common in the ancient world. Kingdoms and peoples made these special agreements with one another to ensure everyone knew the right way to live with each other.

Usually, one of the kingdoms or persons creating a covenant was more powerful than the other. The more powerful group or person usually made the rules for the covenant. We still have copies of ancient covenants and some of them sound a lot like the covenants we find in the Bible.

While the biblical covenants are similar to these other ancient covenants, they are also different. For one thing, the biblical covenants are between a people and their God—not between two kingdoms. God is willing to get involved, even "sign on the dotted line," with those who are willing to do the same with the LORD.

There's one other thing you should know about covenants in the Bible: there are a lot of them! Remember when God promised Noah and all living things that the earth would never again be flooded? That was a covenant. And those different promises God made to Abraham? Those were covenants, too. God also makes a covenant with King David, promising his family and his kingdom would last forever. Later, the prophet Jeremiah spoke of a new covenant God would make with the people.

Throughout the Bible, the LORD is a covenant-making God!

The one with the crossing of the Jordan

HOME

As told by Mark Brett

———

After Moses died, another leader took over. The first generation of people who had escaped slavery from Egypt also passed away. Joshua was told by God to cross over the Jordan River and to take everyone into the lands that would become their home—the lands that stretched from the Great Sea in the west right up to the River Euphrates. Joshua looked around at the ragged bunch of people with him. Somehow they had survived years of wandering in the desert and now there was this river to cross…and not a raft in sight.

Then the LORD said to Joshua, "Tell the priests who carry the Ark of the Covenant to come to the water's edge and stand still in the river." (By the way, this particular Ark wasn't a ship like Noah's, even though in English we call them both arks. This one didn't float.) So the priests carrying the Ark walked to the river's edge and dipped their feet into the water, and—would you believe—the waters rose up into a "heap" (just as they did back at the Sea of Reeds, during the journey from Egypt) so that the people could walk through the dry riverbed without even needing to towel themselves dry. Awesome!

Wait…where did these priests and the Ark of the Covenant come from? They weren't at the Sea of Reeds. Well, the priests and the Ark entered our story in the desert, after Moses had received the Ten Commandments written on two stone tablets. The stone tablets were then placed in the Ark. The weird thing is that no one could open the Ark, so the commandments had to be memorized. In ancient times, lots of laws and stories were passed down from memory, rather than written down and read from books or stone tablets.

Anyway, after years of desert wandering the people were finally home. When they reached the other side of the Jordan, the LORD said to Joshua, "Choose a person from every tribe and have them take a stone from here and stack those stones in a heap at your first campsite after crossing the river. Then, in the years to come, bring your children back here and tell them how the waters parted before the Ark of the Covenant."

So the people did this, and they told their children the stories. Some stories said that only nine and a half of the twelve tribes who crossed the Jordan stayed in Canaan to the west of the river. And where did the other people live? Before he died, Moses had already given two and a half tribes (Reuben, Gad, and half of Manasseh) lands on the east of the Jordan. This eastern territory was shared with a lot of other people, and the River Euphrates was their eastern border.

The two and a half tribes on the east side of the Jordan were worried about being separated from the others. They were concerned that people in the future might say, "God made the Jordan a boundary between us and you, so you Reubenites and Gadites are not part of us any more."

Because of this, the Reubenites and Gadites built an altar to remind everyone that they served the LORD and would continue to keep the laws of Moses. Wherever the tribal groups lived, they were part of the one people.

As time went on, Joshua made covenants with some of the other people who lived in the land of Canaan. Despite the stories where Moses warned the people against making covenants with the locals, Joshua found he had to make some compromises. Joshua took control of the lands that would eventually become the kingdoms of Israel and Judah, but he did not take the land that ran along the coast of the Great Sea—which would become the land of the Philistines. Nor did he take Jerusalem. It would be a long time before the Ark arrived in Jerusalem. (That wouldn't happen until the time of King David.)

Toward the end of his life, Joshua gathered all the tribes together again. He made a special agreement with everyone who met together at Shechem and promised to serve the same God. The people promised Joshua that they would serve the LORD and not other gods. Joshua made a covenant with the people, and he made laws and judgments for them at Shechem. So it wasn't just Moses who made the laws of Israel—Joshua did as well.

For Joshua, not all of the laws of Moses could be applied in practice. Whether they were written on stone or on scrolls or memorized, the laws of God were always on the move!

For "All the Nation"

The stories in the book of Joshua have loose ends—we are not reading the daily news of Canaan written on clay tablets. (If only we could find such tablets buried somewhere!) The stories in Joshua were written on scrolls that were copied and updated.

They were written for "all the nation," but what does that mean exactly? These stories were adapted for the communities who lived in many different places at many different times. New bits were added to the older stories as they were passed down over the generations to families scattered far and wide. And the stories were told to children. We can picture them, perhaps sitting around a campfire near the Jordan River.

The people who lived east of the Jordan were often a very long way from Shechem, the big city in the north of Canaan. And the northern tribes lived quite separately from the southern groups for much of the time, also when Jerusalem was the capital of Judah.

For many ancient Jews, Joshua became a story for "all the nation," but the Samaritans in the north were eventually seen as a separate people even when they shared the same laws of Moses.

The one with Deborah and Jael

WHEN JUDGES JUDGED

As told by Erin H. Moon

Israel was a land of palm trees, but Deborah's Palm Tree was special. Towering like a giantess over its brothers and sisters, you could see it standing tall from a mile away. Its leaves were the size of tents and when the winds came through, the shade they made doubled on the ground below. Everyone knew where it was, so you could say, "Meet me at Deborah's Palm Tree," and all the tribespeople immediately understood what you meant.

When Deborah the judge sat under her palm tree, everyone paid attention. From her spot at the base of the trunk, she commanded respect and admiration. Deborah settled arguments fairly, she led and protected the people, and she was known for her deep connection with God. The people even had a nickname for her: the Torch, because she was fiery and passionate and would do anything to lead them through challenging times.

And the people Israel were in such a time. Because the people forgot their covenant with God, they were ruled by King Jabin of Canaan and his cruel general, Sisera. Just the name Sisera made people tremble in fear, for he commanded 900 powerful chariots and treated Israel harshly for twenty years. Nothing, it seemed, would stop his reign of terror.

One day Deborah summoned her friend, a man named Barak, to see her at the palm tree. She spoke plainly to Barak, like good friends can, "God is ordering you to take your soldiers and climb Mount Tabor. I will help you by herding Sisera and his men to a spot where their chariots will get stuck in the muddy river basin, and then you can defeat them all." She said this with confidence because she and God were friends and Deborah trusted her Friend.

Barak believed in God, and he believed in Deborah, but he was afraid of Sisera. With half a courageous heart and half shaking in his sandals, he told her, "I'll go if you go, but if you don't, I don't think I can do it." Deborah agreed but warned Barak that he would not be remembered for defeating Sisera. That honor would belong to someone else.

So Barak and his soldiers went up to the mountain. And when Sisera heard of this, he gathered all his chariots and warriors and followed them. Deborah held up her end of the deal, and Barak remembered another reason they called her the Torch: she could burn through an army like fire. Deborah and her fighters pushed Sisera into the wetlands and sure enough, those heavy chariots were useless against the mud and the muck. She gave Barak the signal and called, "God has gone before you." Then all of Sisera's warriors and chariots were destroyed, and only one escaped the sword: Sisera himself.

Sisera ran, knowing if Barak or Deborah caught him, he was toast. He came upon the tent of a woman named Jael, who was the wife of a man friendly with King Jabin. Surely I will be safe here, Sisera thought, as Jael pushed back the tent flap and smiled.

"Oh hello, mighty Sisera! You look so tired! You must be exhausted!" Jael welcomed him.

I am so very tired, thought Sisera, his eyes drooping with fatigue. "Please, come inside my tent and rest," she invited him. It looks so very cozy, Sisera thought.

Sisera took the soft blanket Jael offered and the goat's milk she held out to him and he relaxed. The fearsome fighter let his guard down and fell back among the fluffy pillows, a goat's milk mustache whitening his real one. "If anyone comes looking for me," he yawned, "Don't tell them I'm here," his words fading as he drifted into a deep sleep.

What Sisera did not know was that Jael was not like her husband. He may have been friendly with King Jabin, but she was not. Jael stood over the formerly unbeatable general, watching him breathe in and out. Then she tiptoed to pick up a tent peg and hammer, and praying a prayer of courage, she placed the sharp end of the tent peg at Sisera's temple.

Swiftly, with great power, she brought the hammer down with such force that it broke through the general's skull, pushed through his brain, and pinned him to the ground. Sisera died immediately—he didn't even know what hit him. Jael stepped back and took a sip of her goat's milk, satisfied with a job well done.

A few moments later, Barak came up to Jael's camp. He was nervous, knowing that Jael's husband was friends with King Jabin, but he had his orders from the Torch and from God.

"You must be looking for Sisera," Jael said, emerging from her tent, wiping the blood off her hands. "Come inside and I'll show you what you've been searching for." Barak stood, open-mouthed, blinking at the very dead general, and remembered what Deborah had said: that he wouldn't be the one to kill Sisera, and it wouldn't be his name that everyone remembered. That honor belonged to Jael. The people were finally free.

Deborah's Song

When big things happened, the people Israel wanted to remember. And the best way to remember was to write a song. Songs were one way ancient people shared their stories.

One of the oldest parts of the Bible—even older than the story that was written to remember Deborah and Jael—is the song that was sung to remember the day they defeated Sisera. We now know it as Deborah's Song, and it sounded a little like this:

"God raised up two fierce mothers
Willing to do anything for their children.
God's people followed their fiery mother
into battle
And the chariots of their enemies
were destroyed.
And then their blessed second mother
killed the mighty warrior, Sisera,
While his own mother waited and
worried for him to come home.
But he's never coming home, because of
Barak and Deborah and Jael.
Because they came when God called.
the rain came down and bowed before the
God of Israel.
We are finally free because God is with
us and we will forever tell the story."

47

The one where God warns the people

THE PEOPLE WANT A KING

As told by Cynthia Shafer-Elliott

The last judge of the tribes of Israel was a man named Samuel, who also was a prophet. Samuel was a good man, and the people of Israel trusted him. When Samuel's sons grew up, they wanted to be leaders like their dad. But his sons were dishonest and took advantage of their power. The people of Israel did not trust Samuel's sons.

One day, the people of Israel came to Samuel and told him that they did not want his sons to lead them. Instead, they wanted to be like everyone else—to have a king rule over them. Samuel was shocked!

When Samuel prayed to God about what the people wanted, God told Samuel to listen to them. God said that the people were rejecting God as their king, not Samuel as their leader. But! God also told Samuel to warn the Israelites about the ways of a king—to tell them that kings become so powerful, they take advantage of their people and do not treat them well.

Samuel delivered God's message to the people. He told them that they could have a king, but he warned them about the power a king would wield. Samuel gave the Israelites some examples of how a king could misuse their power in ways that would directly affect them. A king could force the people's sons to be his soldiers, build his weapons, and work on his farms. A king could make the people's daughters work in the palace as bakers, cooks, and perfumers. A king could take the best of the people's produce and animals. A king could even take their land. Basically, a king could become so powerful that the people of Israel would be enslaved by him.

But the Israelites did not listen to Samuel's warning—they still wanted a king.

Samuel heard the people and told the LORD. "Listen to their voice and put a king over them," replied God.

Sometime later the LORD revealed to Samuel who should be the first king. God said, "Tomorrow I will send you a man from the land of Benjamin, and you shall make him ruler over my people Israel."

The next day Samuel saw a young, tall, and handsome man, and God said, "That's the guy I was telling you about!" The man's name was Saul and he was looking for his father's donkeys, which had escaped from the family farm. Samuel assured Saul his donkeys had found their way home and invited him to a big feast he had prepared for him.

The next day Samuel told Saul that he would be king. Now it was Saul's turn to be shocked! Samuel poured oil over Saul's head and kissed him, anointing Saul as king in private.

Or did he? Because sometime later, Samuel invited all the people to a town called Mizpah, in the land of Judah. Samuel said to them, "God says, 'I brought you out of Egypt and away from Pharaoh, who was oppressing you. But now you have rejected me and you want a king to rule over you. So line up, and let's do this.'"

The people cast lots, which means they threw something like dice on the ground and how the die landed showed them what God wanted. It kinda sounded like God hadn't already told Samuel that Saul was going to be king! But anyway, lots were cast and each time God's choice became a little clearer: Samuel first called up the tribe of Benjamin, then the family of the Matrites, then the family of Kish, then finally Saul. (Surprise!) But Saul couldn't be found! They finally found Saul hiding behind some baggage!

When Saul came forward, Samuel told the people this was the man God had chosen to be king. "Long live the king!" the people shouted happily. Samuel told Saul and all of the people about the rules of being king. Then Samuel anointed Saul as king in front of everyone and there was much rejoicing.

Now that the Israelites had the king that they wished for, Samuel wanted to remind them about how he led them in an honest way and about all the good things the LORD did for them. Samuel also warned the Israelites that even with a king, they must still worship the LORD alone and obey the LORD's commandments.

But so must the king! Just because a person is king, it doesn't mean that they are above obeying the LORD. In fact, the king has even more responsibility to the LORD and to the people because of their powerful position.

But just as Samuel warned the people, the kings became very powerful and they did not always use their power well.

Ancient Kings

Throughout many kingdoms in the ancient world, people believed kings had a very special relationship with the gods—one that other people, like bakers and farmers and midwives, did not have. In some places, like Egypt, people thought the king actually was a god, while others, like Israel, saw the king as the adopted son of the gods. And still others, like the Mesopotamians, thought the king was appointed by the gods to be their official representative to other people.

Because of their special status and power, kings had special responsibilities. It was thought that the gods gave kings wisdom, which the king was supposed to use to rule with justice and mercy.

They were expected to make laws that were fair and that protected their people. Kings were also in charge of the armies and were responsible for defending and expanding the kingdom. Finally, the king was expected to protect and support the house (or temple) of the gods and the worship that took place there.

Some storytellers in the Bible thought kings were great, and others did not think they were a good idea at all. (We can hear both in this story.) But all of them believed that the kings were meant to "walk in the ways of the LORD," and when they didn't, well...some believed bad things would happen. And not just to the king, but to all of the people.

The one where David gets it wrong

EVERY KING NEEDS A PROPHET

As told by Ellen Davis & Morley van Yperen

———————

Remember how Samuel warned the people that a king might use his power to treat other people badly? Well, that is exactly what happened.

God intended Israel's king to be different from the rulers in other countries. The king was meant to be obedient to God and to lead the people like a wise and gentle shepherd. God appointed prophets to help the kings listen for what God might be saying, and to guide them in following God's will. But Saul did not listen well, and so God turned away from him and chose another king, the shepherd David, who was a man after God's own heart. God showed favor to the young king; David's kingdom grew strong, and he had rest from his enemies on every side.

When David had been king for a long time, he got used to having people do whatever he told them to do. He sent his soldiers off to fight wars and conquer cities, so that he could have even more power. But he did not go into the battlefield with his army. Instead, David stayed safely in his big, comfortable palace in Jerusalem.

But David was not really safe, even at home, for his own heart had turned away from God. Now he thought only about what he wanted and how to get it. Sometimes what David wanted was wrong, but because he was king, no one stood in his way. One day he saw Bathsheba, a beautiful woman who lived near his palace, and he wanted her for his wife. But Bathsheba was already married to Uriah, David's friend since youth and one of the very best soldiers in his army. Even so, King David arranged for Uriah to be killed in battle, so he would never know that David had stolen his wife from him.

But God knew what David had done, and it was evil in God's eyes. God sent the prophet Nathan to confront the king with his sin. Nathan was a wise man, and he knew the best way to touch David's heart. He told him a story. It went like this:

> "There were two men living in the same town; one was rich, and the other one was poor.
>
> The rich man's fields were full of sheep and goats and cattle, while the poor man had just one little ewe lamb, which he had raised in his own house, along with his children. She shared his bit of bread and drank from his cup. She slept in his bed and he loved her like a daughter.
>
> Now one day a traveler came to the home of the rich man. The rich man needed to cook a big welcome dinner, but he decided to spare his own sheep and goats and cattle. Instead he took the poor man's ewe lamb and cooked it for his guest."

When David heard this story, he became hot with rage. "By God," he cried, "that man deserves to die! He must pay for the lamb four times over, because he had no pity."

Then Nathan said, "That man is you! This is what God is saying: 'Because you ignored Me and stole Uriah's wife for yourself, there will be trouble and sadness in your own house and in your own family, from now on.'"

David knew that the prophet had spoken truly. "I have sinned against God," he said. He prayed that God might forgive him and make him a kinder and more faithful person:

> "Give me a pure heart, O God, and a spirit that is right with You."

God never abandoned David, and in time a child was born to Bathsheba and David. His name was Solomon, which means "The Peaceful One," and God loved him. One day, Solomon would inherit his father's royal throne. He would reign as king for many years and build a beautiful temple, God's house in Jerusalem. Like David, Solomon sometimes made bad mistakes; he was not always wise and kind. But that is another story.

PROVERBS

The ones about wisdom

PROVERBIAL ANIMAL FARM

As told by Katharine Dell

Solomon's farm was a large and sprawling one. There were fields for the sheep, a yard where the dog and the goats chased and played, and various ramshackle outbuildings.

Solomon was up early every morning tending his animals—he knew their needs (Prov 12:10) and he tilled his land so that it produced good food (Prov 12:11). He wasn't rich and he wasn't poor. "Better a little with righteousness," he would say, "than worrying about amassing money" (Prov 16:8). He was wise and caring, and he had a feel for the needs of his animals. He knew that any day his luck might run out—"nothing lasts forever" (Prov 27:24). He appreciated the wool provided by his sheep and the milk his goats produced (Prov 27:26-27). He took nothing for granted and saw the hand of God in his life (Prov 16:1).

His animals though were very different—they had opinions and they tended to argue. Take the pig, for example—she was vain. She had a smart gold ring in her snout which gave her a unique beauty, in her eyes anyway (Prov 11:22). Farmer Solomon scolded her, "What's the good of preening yourself all day when you should be fattening yourself up and raising the piglets?" But the pig took no notice and thought she knew better (Prov 25:12).

One day she looked in the cracked old mirror in her stall and noticed that her gold ring was gone. "Oh no, my beauty is spoiled," she wailed.

So who had taken the ring? The pig immediately suspected her neighbors—always argue your case with your neighbor directly (Prov 25:9-10). So she asked the horse.

"Nothing to do with me," he said as he beat his hooves against the side of his stall. "When will I see some action?" he asked. "I'm ready for battle (Prov 21:31), but my energy is being wasted on this farm—and then to be accused of stealing!"

"I agree," said the donkey. "I have to wear this uncomfortable bridle when I'm out in the field—it's a fool's game. What do I get out of it? (Prov 26:3) And the insult!"

The ox joined in—"I may be strong enough to carry a ring, but I am proud of my strength. I've no time for a false friend who accuses me—I'm busy plowing crops." (Prov 14:4).

Then they all said to the pig, "We are faithful witnesses to the truth and we don't lie (Prov 14:5), so don't you accuse us!"

The pig looked around her stall. The ants were scurrying around, always marching up and down, never tiring, always busy. Could they have carried the ring off?

The pig felt tired watching them—another lie down perhaps before challenging them, she thought lazily (Prov 6:6). But, "No!," They said. "We couldn't even lift such a heavy ring—not guilty!"

How about the birds then, that regularly perched on the yard door? The pig had heard that precious things could be swiftly carried off by a calculating bird (Prov 23:4-5), keen to stray and build a bigger nest elsewhere (Prov 27:8). A passing raven stopped—"I hope you are not accusing me," he said, "or I'll peck your eye out for mocking me!" (Prov 30:17).

The pig became sad and stopped eating. She was comforted by her one remaining friend, the moth, who told her sorrow can gnaw away and make holes in your heart (Prov 25:20). "I have no beauty without my ring," the pig sighed. "What is the point of living?" (Prov 16:22).

Farmer Solomon noticed her decline. He brought the dog to see her, and the dog offered her advice: "Don't keep harping on the same problem," she said. "If you return to your vomit, you are stupid. Move on!" (Prov 26:11).

But Farmer Solomon was more sympathetic. "It's okay pig. I can give you another ring, but learn this—there are more important things in life than rings or your looks or even the wealth it gives you; there is friendship (Prov 17:9). Look at the animals that you have hurt by accusing them of wrongdoing. (Prov 13:2) Can't you all get on together and enjoy our wonderful life on the farm? There are no easy answers in life and our knowledge will only get us so far (Prov 1:7)—it is a deeper wisdom that comes from treating yourself and others well that helps us to live harmoniously. Give me vegetables to eat every time if love is at home, rather than fine foods and arguments among my animals (Prov 15:17)!"

The pig thought for a moment then said, "You are right, farmer. Anxiety weighs down the heart, but a good word cheers us all up!" (Prov 12:25) When she next saw her animal neighbors she apologized, "I've been a fool (Prov 26:4). Please forgive me." And they did.

So no longer did the pig prance and preen and set herself over others, but she took time for her friends and got on with helping Farmer Solomon in her own, uniquely piggy way.

What is Wisdom?

The proverbs in the book of Proverbs give us advice on what it means to be wise and how to avoid "folly" or foolishness.

Well, not "us" exactly. The book of Proverbs, just like the rest of the Bible, wasn't written with "us" in mind. These poetic sayings were collected from as far away as Egypt to help teach wealthy ancient Israelite boys, who were being educated to help rule the kingdom. Which is why some proverbs might not make much sense to us today.

But even today there is wisdom for us in Proverbs. One of the most important things Proverbs teaches us about wisdom is that being wise isn't as easy as following a set of rules. What might be wise in one situation, could be foolish in another.

To make sure we don't miss this point, the storytellers placed two opposite proverbs right next to each other...

"Do not answer fools according to their folly, lest you become a fool yourself." (Prov 26:4)

"Answer fools according to their folly, lest they think themselves wise." (Prov 26:5)

Tricky, right?! Wisdom involves responding to each situation as that situation requires, which is why there are no shortcuts on the path to wisdom.

The one with Israel and Judah

A KINGDOM DIVIDED

As told by Dan McClellan

Some stories don't really have any heroes. Or if they do have heroes, they turn out to be villains in the end. This makes for a sad story, but there can be a lot to learn in these kinds of stories. 1 Kings 11 and 12 is the beginning of a story like this. It explains how the kingdom of Israel was divided into two separate kingdoms. In the north would be the kingdom of Israel, and in the south would be the kingdom of Judah. (You should know that the people telling us this story were part of the kingdom of Judah, and so this story is told from their point of view.)

The story begins with someone who seems like they could be the hero—a man named Jeroboam ben Nebat, who was a servant of King Solomon and came from the land of Israel in the north. Jeroboam was a strong man who impressed the king while he was working for him in Jerusalem. To reward him, Solomon made him the leader of the enforced workers in his northern homeland of Ephraim. But Jeroboam would end up rebelling against Solomon's kingdom. Here's how it happened...

After his father David died, Solomon ruled from Jerusalem for many years. Solomon built a big and beautiful temple—a house for the LORD—in Jerusalem, and it became famous throughout the lands. But over time, God became angry with Solomon because he had too many wives from foreign lands who worshipped other gods, and Solomon's heart began to turn away from God. God wanted to take Solomon's kingdom away from him. But God still loved Solomon's father David, so God told Solomon that he would be able to keep his kingdom until he died. That sounds like a pretty good deal! But Solomon didn't think so.

One day, as Jeroboam was heading back home from Jerusalem, a prophet named Ahijah met him on the road. Ahijah said God would take Solomon's kingdom away from him and give the ten tribes of Israel to Jeroboam. These tribes were Asher, Dan, Ephraim, Gad, Issachar, Manasseh, Naphtali, Reuben, Simeon, and Zebulun. The other two tribes, Judah and Benjamin, would stay with Solomon's family. God said this wouldn't happen right away, though: Solomon would be allowed to rule as king until he died. If Jeroboam would obey God when he became king, his kingdom would be as great as David's.

When Solomon heard about this, he got upset and tried to kill Jeroboam. But Jeroboam ran away and hid.

When Solomon died, his son, Rehoboam, wanted to become king. He went to Shechem in the north to be made king by the people. Jeroboam could have refused to recognize Rehoboam as king, but he didn't! He and the people who followed him weren't in love with power. They just wanted a righteous king. They promised Rehoboam that if he would be kind to them, they would keep being his servants. Rehoboam wanted to think about it, so he told the people to come back in three days for his answer.

Meanwhile, Rehoboam went and asked for advice. The older people his father had trusted said he should be kinder to the people than his father was. This way the people would be happy to serve him. The younger people who grew up with Rehoboam said being kinder than his father would make him look like a weak king. They said he should be nastier to the people than his father was. Rehoboam liked that idea. He ignored the advice of the older people and he threatened to be even nastier to Jeroboam and his followers.

The people of Israel did not like the way Rehoboam treated them. They decided that they did not want to be a part of Rehoboam's kingdom anymore. When King Rehoboam came with one of his officials to the north, the people killed his official and chased the king all the way back to Jerusalem. Rehoboam was now only king over the south—Judah (and Benjamin, although the story doesn't mention that part). The people of the north made Jeroboam their king, finally fulfilling God's promise. With Jeroboam as king, the northern kingdom of Israel became a very wealthy kingdom that traded with the nations all around it. But Jeroboam wouldn't remain the hero for long.

Jeroboam didn't want his people to travel to the southern kingdom of Judah, ruled by Rehoboam, to worship God in the temple at Jerusalem, so he had temples made in cities at the north and south of his kingdom named Dan and Bethel. He made two gold calves and put them in the temples. Then he held feasts and offered sacrifices.

One day a man of God from Judah came and warned Jeroboam that he was turning away from God. God would destroy the kingdom of Israel if he did not stop. Jeroboam promised he would stop, but after the man of God left, Jeroboam did not stop. The story ends by telling us that because of this, Jeroboam's kingdom would be destroyed. The kingdoms of Israel and Judah would never again be united as one kingdom.

AMOS; 2 KINGS 17

The one with the fall of Israel

HERE COMES TROUBLE

As told by Deborah Winters

Have you ever visited another school, or neighborhood, or maybe even a different country and felt like you were a stranger in a strange land? When I, Amos, was first called by God to go to the northern kingdom of Israel, I was considered a stranger, but soon many of the people I was speaking to would become strangers in a strange land.

To be honest, even the folks in the southern kingdom of Judah where I grew up thought I was a little "strange" because I talked and listened to God. They called me "Amos the prophet." Back when I still lived in Judah, I was a shepherd who also tended figs on sycamore trees in Tekoa. (Can you find Tekoa on the map in the last story?)

Sometimes I would thank God for the beauty of the sunrise, or ask God for the protection of my flock, and sometimes I would simply tell God what was bothering me. Have you ever tried talking to God about what upsets you? God is a GREAT listener!

God would speak to me in visions, pictures, and images that had a message. That's how I ended up in Israel. God told me to leave my home and go share God's visions with our rival, the northern kingdom of Israel

From every outward appearance, the northern kingdom looked prosperous. They had made clever partnerships with other countries and used the trade routes within their borders to their advantage. The problem was that they got wealthy by taking advantage of the poor and oppressing the needy. They considered themselves holy because they worshipped God, but they also worshipped other gods and tried to silence God's prophets. They thought they were safe and secure, but I was sent to tell them that God had

had enough of their evil ways. Because they had not changed their behavior and followed only God, they would lose everything.

I got their attention when I spoke to them using the pattern, "for three sins and for four." I told them that God was going to bring justice to their neighbors: Syria, Philistia, Tyre, Edom, Ammon, and Moab (Can you find some of these on the map?).

At the name of each enemy territory, the crowd began chanting with me "for three sins and for four" and couldn't wait to hear the justice God was going to dish out to their enemies.

They were surprised when I included "for three sins and for four" of the southern kingdom of Judah, my homeland, and they cheered even louder.

Then I turned the tables on them and said "for three sins and for four" God was unhappy with the northern kingdom of Israel because they sold righteous people for money, poor people for a pair of sandals, and denied justice to those who needed it most. Their only hope was in repentance (turning back to God and following God's ways) and because they had not repented, now only a small remnant would be saved.

I warned them that God was like a roaring lion and the northern kingdom was God's prey. I shared the visions God had given me of the bowl full of the last of the summer fruit, the oncoming locust army, and the measuring line which found them way out of line. The Day of the LORD was coming, and it would not be a joyous day (as some thought), but a day of judgement, for God hated their empty worship, festivals, offerings, and praise songs.

They thought they were something special because God saved Israel from Egypt, but I reminded them that God also saved the Philistines from Caphtor and the Arameans from Kir. Because of their evil ways, God's justice would come upon them like water rushing down a mountain and there would be no stopping God's righteousness.

I would love to tell you that they listened to me, but instead their priest Amaziah told me to stop causing trouble and go prophesy in my own country. I told him, because he would not listen to me, he would lose everything.

When the Assyrian armies attacked, all those who could not run to the southern kingdom of Judah or other places of safety, were either killed or taken to Assyria. The Assyrians settled other people in the lands of the northern kingdom, so now it was full of strangers. And the people of the northern kingdom? Well, now they were living as strangers in strange lands.

Still, God provided. In the past, God sent prophets to remind the people of the southern kingdom of Judah to take care of the orphans and the widows. Now the prophets reminded the people to care for the strangers who lived among them as well—the refugees from what once was, and never again would be, the northern kingdom of Israel.

The Ten Lost Tribes

The northern kingdom of Israel and the southern kingdom of Judah were not the only kingdoms in the ancient world. There were many other kingdoms and some of them were very big indeed. Some were so big we call them "empires", and one of these empires was Assyria.

Assyria was so very big and so very powerful that the smaller kingdoms nearby—kingdoms like Israel and Judah—had to pay them money. If they did not, Assyria would send their armies to attack the people and take their land.

King Hoshea of Israel decided to stop paying money to Assyria. He hoped the king of Egypt, another powerful empire, would help protect Israel from Assyria.

But Egypt's pharaoh did not, and Assyria attacked Israel. The Assyrians took King Hoshea and the Israelites captive, moving them to Assyria so that they could move other peoples into the lands that used to be called Israel. To this day, the ten tribes of Israel are known as the ten lost tribes.

The refugees from the northern kingdom who made it safely to the southern kingdom of Judah shared their stories with their new neighbors. The stories they brought with them influenced the southern kingdom's leaders and storytellers. So much so, that the people of the southern kingdom of Judah began to be known by the name Israel.

JONAH

The one with Jonah

YOU WANT ME TO DO WHAT?!

As told by Jione Havea

───────────

Jonah's people were troubled by the empire of Assyria. So troubled that when the people spoke of Assyria, they trembled. They pictured thundering chariots, people screaming, babies crying, and animals running in all directions. They pictured smoke and fire and broken fields. Destruction. They pictured the end of everything they had ever known. Despair.

So, when God told Jonah to go up to Nineveh, the capital of Assyria, to tell them to stop their wicked ways, Jonah had a very good reason to not want to go. If he went to Nineveh, that would have been like going to the home of a bully.

Instead of going up to Nineveh, Jonah fled down to Joppa, away from God. He found a ship going out to Tarshish—which was VERY far away. He paid his ticket, boarded the ship, and went down to the belly of the ship.

But God saw him sleeping among the baggage, so God sent a big storm to bully the sea and toss the ship around. The storm was supposed to wake Jonah up and bring him out of hiding. But Jonah did not wake up. The captain came down and shook him, shouting, "What are you doing?! Get up and call on your god!"

The storm was not in the weather forecast, and it was so big that the ship thought about breaking up. The sailors were afraid that the ship might sink. They could drown!

The captain and the crew cast lots and figured out that the storm came because Jonah did something bad. The captain and crew prayed to Jonah's God and then they did what Jonah recommended: they picked Jonah up and threw him into the sea. Yes, Jonah had asked to be thrown into the troubled sea. WEIRD.

Miraculously, as soon as Jonah fell into the waters, the sea calmed down. The crew and passengers were amazed, and they thanked God with promises and gifts.

Meanwhile, in the sea, Jonah was sinking like he did not know how to swim. God saw and sent a big fish up to rescue Jonah. This big fish had no hands, but it had a big belly—so it swallowed Jonah! The big fish swallowed but did not bite Jonah, and Jonah did not die in the belly of the fish. For three days and three nights, Jonah waited in the watery depths. He thanked God with praises and promises while he was in the belly of the fish.

Then the big fish vomited Jonah out. EEEEEEEEWWWWWWW.

Jonah landed on dry land somewhere close to Nineveh—with all the fishy stuff stuck on him. "Get up," the LORD said. Jonah had no choice but to go up to Nineveh, as God wanted in the first place. He had to do what he did not want to do.

Nineveh was a big city, with many people, children, and animals. Jonah arrived and started to preach, "In forty days Nineveh will be overthrown!" The whole city believed him. They changed their behaviors because they did not want God to be angry with them. Their king heard what they did, and he joined them. Everyone—even the animals!—fasted and put on sackcloth to show God that they had stopped being wicked and were sorry.

God saw that Nineveh had made the right choice, so God's mind changed about Nineveh. God decided to not trouble them. Why? Because the people, children, animals, and king of Nineveh were doing the right thing.

Jonah was not happy with God letting Nineveh off the hook. He still pictured the thundering chariots and broken fields. He wanted God to punish these Assyrians. Jonah told God that what just happened was the reason he fled the first time. He knew that if Nineveh was sorry, God would let Nineveh off. Jonah was so mad that he wanted to die.

He stormed out of the city. He made a booth, sat in its shade, and waited to see what would happen. Whose side would God take—Jonah's side or Nineveh's side?

God let a bush grow over Jonah, to give him some comfort. Jonah was very happy with the bush. But the next morning God sent a worm to attack the bush. Just like that, the bush dried up. When the sun came up, it burned

Jonah so badly that he again wanted to die. He complained, and asked God to let him die. Jonah was SO very angry that the bush was destroyed, but that God did not destroy the Assyrians of Nineveh—the worst enemy of Jonah's people.

But God said to Jonah, "Just as you were concerned for the bush, which you did not grow, so much more am I concerned for Nineveh, the great city, in which there are many people and many animals." Yes, God cared for Jonah *and* for Nineveh *and* the animals.

HABAKKUK

The one where Judah looks like Israel

HERE COMES TROUBLE...AGAIN

As told by Anna Sieges Beal

———————

All around the prophet Habakkuk, people were getting away with things. They would lie, cheat, steal, and hurt one another and no one stopped them. Worst of all, they knew better. Habakkuk and these people lived in Judah. Judahites were supposed to be honest, fair, generous, and peaceful. That was God's way, but when Habakkuk looked around, he only saw cruelty. With his hands balled into fists and his eyes screwed shut, he yelled at God.

> "How long are you going to make me look at these cheaters? They are bullies, and you are doing nothing to stop them! My heart is breaking. I need you to help, God! Answer me!"

God understood that Habakkuk was tired, angry, and filled with sadness. God was filled with sadness too, because of the Judahites' behavior. So God showed Habakkuk what would happen soon. God answered,

> "Look at that powerful country across the desert, between the two mighty rivers. Do you see those people called Babylonians? They are ruthless. They never show pity or compassion. They mock everyone who tries to stop them. Your king and all his strongest soldiers won't even slow them down. They capture nations like a net catches fish. They are coming to Judah, Habakkuk, and no one will escape, not even in Jerusalem."

Habakkuk was not happy about this message, so he argued with God.

"God, I thought you were good! Why would you send those
heartless Babylonians to Judah, where they will destroy everything?
I thought you hated that kind of evil!"

Habakkuk was sick with worry. He could not understand what God had
shown him. He knew what had happened in Israel. Many years earlier, the
prophet Amos had seen greedy people refusing to share with others. They
didn't care that their neighbors were hungry and homeless, they just wanted
more for themselves. So God sent the Assyrians from across the desert to tear
down every wall in Israel until nothing was left.

Habakkuk also remembered what happened years earlier in the
countryside of Judah. The prophet Micah howled and screamed because
powerful people in Judah were taking houses and fields that didn't belong to
them. Making themselves richer, they stole all the farmers' harvests and left
the farmers with nothing. In the end, a foreign king from across the desert
marched to Judah crushing every town and farm. He even came to Jerusalem,
but God saved Jerusalem—that time.

It was all happening again. Habakkuk wanted to tear his hair out! He
needed to get up high for a new perspective. He ran up the stairs leading to
the top of the city wall. Now, he could see for miles. The valleys around the
city rose into hills. Would the Babylonians come over those hills with their
enormous army? They would look like specks at first and then grow into
more soldiers than anyone could count. He looked back into the city. He saw
women and men walking from building to building. Some teachers from the
temple talking as they studied a scroll. Two little girls chasing a goat down
the stone-paved streets. What would happen to them?

Habakkuk crossed his arms over his chest and glared at the temple. Surely
God wouldn't allow Jerusalem's destruction. And then, God replied,

"I am sending the Babylonians. I won't change my mind. You
should write my message down." (In Habakkuk's time, people
didn't write things very often. If they did, it meant the message
was serious and unusual.) "I know this news feels like a heavy
weight on your shoulders. But I promise you, the Babylonians will

not take over the world. They will get what they deserve for all the damage they cause in Judah."

God's words didn't make Habakkuk feel any better. He didn't know what to do. After he wrote God's message, he decided to sing a song he had learned at the temple when he was young:

Oh God, you have always been our hero.
Nothing can stop you, not even the biggest sea monster.
When we are worried that we'll be gobbled up, you always save us.
Even when I have nothing and everything has gone wrong,
Even then, Even then,
I will sing with joy because you love to rescue me.

Prophets

There are three words in ancient Hebrew that are sometimes translated as "prophet" in English. The first is ro'eh, which means "seer," and the second is chozeh, a "visionary." Both of these suggest the prophet can see and understand the world in ways that others cannot.

The third word, navi', means "a person who speaks for God." There's even a whole section of the Bible—Nevi'im, or Prophets—named after them. Look at the yellow thumb tab on the opposite page—you're in that section now!

Prophets are people (women, men, young, old) who have the ability to see things from God's perspective and tell others God's thoughts. Prophets know everything God created is connected: the trees, flowers, rabbits, lizards, and every human. When people hurt God's creation (including one another), prophets name those who are guilty of causing pain and tell them about the consequences for their behavior.

Often, prophets say things that are hard for people to hear, especially people with power. Remember "Every King Needs a Prophet?" Nathan had to tell David that his behavior was wrong. That's what prophets do, they tell everyone the truth, even queens and kings, because they understand God's perspective—that God's creation is precious, and no one should hurt what God has made.

The one with the Babylonians

FOR I KNOW THE PLANS

As told by Alexiana Fry

It seems like everyone has forgotten what happened in Israel. The same things that happened up there keep happening here in Judah. There is injustice everywhere. People are hurting one another and not taking care of each other. Just like in Israel. And look how that turned out. Why does no one remember?

Oh God, this job makes me so sad.

I am young and I do not know how to speak! I am nervous about the work You have given me to do. I was a priest, but You have made me a prophet, too. But I am just Jeremiah! I am so anxious. I hear what has happened in places nearby and it makes me sick with worry. We have been saved from disaster before, but I see what is happening and I have to tell the truth.

We must stop hurting each other and do good instead. We must take care of the strangers, the widows, and the orphans. We must walk in Your ways. Or Babylon will come.

****

Well, that didn't take long. Just like me, our king was young—he could have chosen to do good. Instead he did not protect us. He put on a show and made himself feel important by rebelling against the mighty king of Babylon. I warned King Jehoiakim—quite a few times! I told him we could change and things could be different. But King Jehoiakim decided his reputation was more important than God's, and put all of us in great danger. Then his son, King Jehoiachin, did the same things as his dad.

The Babylonians came. They took everything inside our precious and beautiful temple. They took people from our community far away, to lands they had never been before.

King Jehoiachin was taken from us, too. Babylon put a different king in his place—a man called Zedekiah. I cried so much, it felt like I would just dry up.

****

God, I feel like maybe the people who aren't in their homes anymore—the ones who were taken to a land far away—are crying a lot too, so I wrote them a letter. I hope this letter will encourage them, even though it is okay to be sad. That it will bring them hope, even though everything around them is really hard. That it will remind them that You have not forgotten them, even though they are far away from us and the places they have always known. That it will encourage them to do good and make a home in this new place, and that maybe things will be okay, even though nothing will ever be the same.

****

Many years have passed and even though we have a new king, things in our land are still really bad because King Zedekiah decided he wasn't going to listen to God either. I tried to keep telling the truth, especially when Babylon came back. Because they did come back.

King Zedekiah decided to make friends with Egypt's pharaoh, thinking this would protect us from Babylon, but it just put us in even more danger. My warnings made the king's friend angry. "Jeremiah," he said, "You are siding with Babylon," and he put me in jail. King Zedekiah brought me back out, but made sure he kept an eye on me.

Babylon kept the city of Jerusalem surrounded and we began to run out of food. People were frantic. King Zedekiah told our people to free their fellow Judahites whom they had enslaved. At first they listened and freed our people, but then they took them back and enslaved them all over again! God does not like injustice. Why does no one remember?

The Babylonian army broke through Jerusalem's walls. They captured King Zedekiah.

We had no food and were so weak, but still the army set most of our city on fire and made sure everything was completely destroyed.

And just like the first time, they took people away. They put heavy chains around our people so they could not run away, and made them walk to a far off place.

Just when I thought I would be taken too, the Babylonian king told the captain of his army that I was to stay in Jerusalem (for now).

So many people were forced to leave, and my entire homeland is in ruins. I cried so much for myself and for my people. Nothing will ever be the same. But I keep listening to God.

Exile

Do you remember the very first story in this book? The one where we imagined we were in Jerusalem 2,500 years ago? Well we have returned to where we began—back when the mighty, scary Babylonian army destroyed Jerusalem.

The Babylonian army had one job: to make the Babylonian empire bigger and stronger than it already was. In 598/7 BCE the army marched into Judah and took King Jehoiachin and others into exile, moving them to lands far from their own. People in exile cannot return home without permission and most never get it.

Babylon put a new king on Judah's throne—one they thought would do what they wanted. But around ten years later, the new king wasn't working out for Babylon, so the army came back and took even more people into exile. Among them were priests, scribes, and others from the king's court. Some could read and write, and they knew Judah's laws, history, and stories well.

As you think about the stories we have read together so far, can you see how the questions asked by the priests, scribes, and others who had been taken into exile shaped the stories they gathered and retold? Can you see why they wanted to know why bad things happened? And where God was? And who they were now that they had lost everything?

This is where the Bible began, but the stories do not end here...

PSALMS

The ones where we can be honest with God

ARE YOU THERE GOD?

As told by Joshua James

Have you ever had a prayer in your heart that you were too frightened to pray? Perhaps you were angry with someone and you wanted to ask God to punish them? Perhaps something terrible happened and you wanted to ask God why? Or perhaps you were just mad at God and you were too scared to say it?

Being honest with God can feel scary sometimes. But there's a whole book in the Bible that shows us it's okay to tell God what we're thinking and feeling—no matter how big or scary those feelings might seem. It shows us that God can handle the BIGGEST of big feelings, and that God wants us to share them in prayer. And that book is the book of Psalms.

The book of Psalms is a collection of ancient Israel's poems, prayers, and songs. And there are a lot of them—150! Here's one you may know: "The Lord is my shepherd. I shall not want…" (Ps 23:1).

Many passages in Psalms read like a diary or journal entry, making it seem as if the poet woke up, poured a cup of coffee, opened a notebook at the kitchen table, and began to write something about their life. The psalms feel a bit like a private conversation. But these psalms were probably written for worship services, kind of like the songs people sing or the prayers people read all together in churches and synagogues today. This seems like it could be true, but (like many things in the Bible!) it's hard to know for sure—we don't know who wrote the psalms, or when they did, or why.

Here's something we do know. Psalms includes many different kinds of writings that share many different feelings and experiences. There are psalms that people might have prayed or sung when they were happy…

"Make a joyful noise to the Lord, all the earth. Serve the Lord with gladness; come into his presence with singing." (Ps 100:1)

And there are some for when they were sad...

"I am tired from my moaning; every night I flood my bed with tears" (Ps 6:6)

There are psalms for when they were thankful...

"I give you thanks, O Lord, with my whole heart" (Ps 138:1)

...and some for when they were afraid.

"I am so scared, my body shakes" (Ps 55:5)

There are even psalms for when the people were so mad they couldn't see straight, and when they wanted their enemies to
be punished...

"Happy are they who take my enemies' children and whack them against rocks." (Ps 137:9) Yikes!

...and when they doubted if God cared about them:

"How long, O Lord? Will you forget me forever? How long will you hide your face from me?" (Ps 13)

This is what makes the book of Psalms so special and maybe why so many people love its poetry still. By giving space to all of these prayers and songs, it tells us that we can feel whatever we feel, and we can talk to God about it freely. Nothing is off limits!

Even though the psalms are ancient, there are psalms that describe how we feel right now. Just like the ancient Israelites, there are times when we are happy, or sad, or thankful, or scared, or mad. In fact, some folks think this is what a "life of faith" looks like.

There will be times when everything is okay, when the world works like it should, and when God feels close by. (There are psalms for that.) But there will also be times when everything just feels off. Maybe someone we love gets sick or the news on TV is super scary. In those moments, it's easier to ask questions—to wonder if God is there. (There are psalms for that too.) And then, maybe a little later, things get back to normal, and we are thankful. (Yep. Psalms still has you covered.)

Here's one last thing about psalms that makes them really cool. These poems have been voiced for thousands of years by people all over the world. When we use them for ourselves, right now, we join a massive chorus of people who have been where we are. We are not alone.

So…what do you want to say to God? Psalms says whatever your answer, it's okay.

You Try!

The three main types of psalms we find in our Bible are called praise, lament, and thanksgiving psalms.

A praise psalm celebrates who God is or the big things God has done. A lament psalm tells God about a problem and asks God to fix it. A thanksgiving psalm describes a time when things were rough but God rescued the person praying.

One of the best things about the psalms is that they show us how we can pray our own prayers to God. Let's try it! Finish the sentences below with your own words to create psalms of praise, lament, or thanksgiving. And don't be afraid to be a little silly! I bet God thinks you're really funny.

Praise

God, I praise you because you are …

Even when I am …I will say that you are …

Lament

God, I'm struggling with …

I feel so …

Please help me by …

Thanksgiving

God, thank you for …

Knowing that … is part of my life makes me feel … You're so …, God.

The one where bad things happen to good people

WITH FRIENDS LIKE THESE

As told by Katharine Dell

It was the end of a scorching hot day in Teman, as Eliphaz finished his work and sat down to drink some cooling water. It had been a day like most others except for one piece of news that troubled him: a messenger had come to tell him that his old friend Job was in trouble—something about a series of bad happenings that had led to him losing everything.

"Everything?" he asked the messenger. "What, all those she-asses and camels that he had?"

"Worse," the messenger replied, "Not just his goods and chattels but his lovely children, too—all killed when a roof fell on them."

"My goodness," said Eliphaz, "I must go over and see him. He must be falling apart."

Unbeknown to Eliphaz, two other messengers had set out on the same day, one for Shuah and the other for Naamah, to the homes of two more of Job's old friends, Bildad and Zophar. They were equally stunned—Job was the most God-fearing and righteous man they had ever met. How could such bad things happen to such a good person? They, too, decided to set out and see Job.

The three friends met on the way. As they drew near to Job's city in Uz they saw a large pile of rubbish with a man sitting on the top. "Could that be him?" they asked, looking questioningly at one another. As they drew near they saw that it was indeed Job. Open sores covered his body and they could see that he was in real pain. His clothes were torn and tattered, and his head was shaved as mourning customs dictated. The only member of his family still alive was his wife, who stood nearby but didn't really seem the sympathetic type. "Of course," they said to themselves, "She is suffering just as much in her own way."

What could the friends do? Their first reaction was a good one: just sit with Job in comforting silence. Isn't that what friends do best? Console by your very presence.

But after a week they started to get tetchy—and so did Job. He was lamenting and moaning and wishing he hadn't been born. His friends started to get irritated. They had always been taught that suffering happened when someone did something wrong. So had Job! "Behave well and good things will come to you," he used to say. Now Job was suffering and claiming that he had not done anything wrong—that he had behaved perfectly at every turn. This made no sense to his friends. They told him, "You must have done something bad as God doesn't punish people for no reason."

"No," he replied, "I never did anything wrong—I was a model citizen. Look how I looked after people in the community and helped the poor. I couldn't have done more."

His friends argued back, "No, you must have done something to upset God—maybe you are just not seeing it?"

The arguments started to get fractious. "How worthless you are as comforters," said Job. "How full of windy words you are!" said the friends. "What kind of friends do you call yourselves if all you can do is criticize?" said Job. "How ungrateful," said the friends. "And we came all this way to see you."

So how was it resolved? Well, in the end, God appeared in a whirlwind. Job demanded to know why terrible things had happened when he had been so very good. But God didn't really answer Job's questions, not directly anyway. After all, God created a whole cosmos: who can question God's purposes? And so Job and his friends never found out why bad things happen to good people—it remains a mystery to this day!

But God did express frustration with the way Job's friends had tried to speak on God's behalf. They had done well to comfort Job and sit alongside him, but their arguments became less than helpful. In the end Job forgave them and there was a happily-ever-after ending. Job received twice as many sheep and camels than he had before, and God gave him a new set of children. (You might be wondering whether Job getting a bunch of brand-new kids is a happily-ever-after ending, and you would not be alone!)

And what happened to the friends? Well, we are not told, but we can assume they went back home and reflected on what they had learnt. Perhaps in future they would not be so quick to think they were speaking for God, and maybe they had learnt some wisdom and humility. We can hope so, anyway.

Why Do Bad Things Happen?

Poor Job. If God is so good and powerful, then why do bad things happen? The Bible has lots of answers to this very good question, because lots of terrible things happened to God's people. They had a lot of time to think about it.

When the Assyrians conquered Israel, and then the Babylonians conquered Judah, some of the prophets thought these bad things happened because the people (especially the kings) had turned away from God, and the land was full of injustice and oppression.

In Exodus we are told that when people do something wrong, their grandchildren and even their great-grandchildren are punished. Yikes! But Ezekiel says, "No, everyone is judged for their own actions."

Job gives us another answer altogether. When Job asks God why bad things happened to him, God's very long answer basically says, "You're not God, Job. That's not for you to know." Which is pretty unsatisfying, but very honest.

The Bible gives us lots of answers to this question because there are lots of ways to think about it. But Job's storytellers knew that sometimes the best answer for a really good question is, "We don't know."

The Bible might not give us one answer, but it does show us that we are not alone in asking this very hard question.

The one where nothing really matters

DAYS LIKE THESE

As told by Peter Enns

Seven-year-old Lilah threw down her Taylor Swift school bag and sobbed like her eyes were attached to a water hose.

"What's wrong, Lilah?" asked five-year-old Beau. "Why are you crying?" Beau was very concerned about his big sister, but this just made Lilah cry more! Thankfully, her mother came in right after her.

"Oh, Lilah, my sweetie," she said. "What is happening?"

With crocodile tears running down her cheeks, Lilah said, "Mama, I'm so sad and I'm so mad about school!"

"Whatever happened, my love?"

"Everything went wrong! The picture I drew was so bad! I tried sooooooo hard to make it nice, but it looked ugly. Then, I couldn't read the story in front of the class because I didn't know all the words. Then when we went out to play, I lost every game. I tried SO HARD, but no matter how hard I tried today nothing good happened. It was a STUPID DAY, and everything today was just so STUPID!"

****

Have you ever felt like Lilah felt? Maybe you've had days that made you sad and mad. This happens to everybody. It happens to grown-ups, too! And you know what? It even happened to people in the Bible!

One of these people is a man named Qohelet. We don't know much about him, other than he was a grown-up and was even a king! But that's about it. In fact, Qohelet isn't even his name. He used a fake name. Maybe he wanted to keep his real name a secret? He had some things to say that not everyone would want to hear. Maybe that's why he used a fake name.

Like Lilah, Qohelet thought nothing mattered. No matter what he did, he felt it didn't mean anything. And do you know what else? He was sad about this, and even mad—and he was especially mad at God!

Many people think that it is wrong to be mad at God, but Qohelet didn't care. He just had all these feelings that he couldn't hold in anymore. So he wrote words and words about how nothing matters, and that it is God's fault for making a world where nothing makes sense.

Qohelet was very brave and honest. And as we see in the book he wrote (which we call Ecclesiastes), God never gets mad at him. And many people came to see that he was a wise teacher! Qohelet loved God and himself enough to be completely honest about his feelings.

So what did Qohelet say that was so brave and honest? Well, the first words he speaks are, "Everything is *hevel*." You might not know that word because it is a word in Hebrew, the language Qohelet spoke. It means something like fog or a wisp of smoke. So when Qohelet says that everything is *hevel*, he means that everything will wind up not mattering. It's like fog that is there in the morning, but then disappears when the sun rises. Or like the smoke from a candle. Blow out the candle, and then what happens? Smoke rises from the wick—at first there is a lot but soon the smoke is so thin you can barely see it. And then it is gone.

That is what Qohelet said about life. It's just like a foggy morning or smoke from a candle—sooner or later it is not there anymore. Nothing we do matters because everything is like fog or candle smoke. That's how he felt, and so he was honest about it.

Qohlelet was not happy at all. He was sad, mad, and probably scared. But he was not going to hold it in. He said what he was feeling, just like Lilah did when she came home from school.

Did you notice that neither Beau nor Lilah's mother told her to stop crying? They let Lilah show her feelings because they love her and care for her. God loves us and our feelings. God wants us all to be honest and not feel like we have to pretend everything is okay when it is not. It is okay to be sad and mad, even with God! God does not want us to be fake. God understands and cares for us.

Some days we are happy. Some days we feel like nothing matters no matter how hard we try. Both days matter to God. God cares for all our days.

HAGGAI

The one where the exiles return

HOME, AGAIN

As told by Steed Vernyl Davidson

Many years ago, our city was in a war with the Babylonians. When the Babylonian army came to our city of Jerusalem they destroyed homes, fields, the king's palace, and the temple. They killed people. They took away many people to Babylon—the king's family, our priests, our scribes, and others they decided were important. And they left the small farmers like me behind.

For years, we farmers kept the city going and tried to worship on the ruins of the temple.

When a new Persian king came to power and defeated the Babylonians, he told our people who lived in Babylon that they could come home to Jerusalem, if they wanted to. This was the news they had waited all those long years in exile for. Home!

They came back with different names and different ideas. Some of them came with the idea to rebuild the city. They started with their homes and the city walls. And next they wanted to rebuild the temple.

The prophet Haggai was one of these people. When he came home, he started preaching in the city. He believed God wanted him to make sure we rebuilt the temple. Most of the city was in ruins, and Haggai believed that we had the support of the Persian king to rebuild. So Haggai spent a lot of time encouraging us to rebuild the temple.

Not everyone thought rebuilding the temple was a good idea. Some said the time was not right, because they didn't know whether God was still angry with us. They thought that if they rebuilt the temple and God was still angry with us, then the temple could be destroyed again. Others were too busy rebuilding their own homes to spend time on a project that they didn't see was of benefit to them.

Haggai pleaded with Zerubbabel, our governor, and Joshua, the priest in charge. He wanted them to see that rebuilding the temple would change things in the city.

He begged the people to see how things could turn around. For years we lived a difficult life in Jerusalem. We had droughts and little food to go around. Most of us were farmers and didn't harvest much from our fields. Haggai believed that if we focused on rebuilding the temple, God would be pleased. And life could be better in the city.

About a month after he started preaching, Haggai asked the people what we remembered of the old temple, the one that was destroyed. Many just looked at the ground and didn't answer him. No one said they missed having a temple. Maybe they forgot about the festivals that took place there and the celebrations that brought the community together. Maybe they were so beaten down by life they had little room to find joy. Maybe they didn't see a place for the glory of God in a city filled with rubble. Or maybe they couldn't remember because they had never seen the temple. They might have been the children and grandchildren of people sent into exile, who had lived their whole lives in faraway lands.

But Haggai was not discouraged. He believed rebuilding the temple was the most important thing that could happen in the city. He continued to encourage the people—
those of us whose families lived in the city all the years since the war and those who had recently come back. He said that we should be confident that God was with us. He told us that we should remember how God was with our ancestors when they left Egypt. We should not be afraid. Haggai worked so hard to get us to believe again.

Haggai went to the priests, and they talked about what it meant to have a temple in the city. The temple would remind people of God. In the temple, we could perform rituals to mark important activities in our life. Building the temple gave us the chance to experience some good in our city.

Perhaps we would have better harvests. Maybe we would have more oil for celebrations. And people would start to believe in themselves and expect a better future. Since the war, most people were so sad and depressed. A temple where we could celebrate might bring us together as a community.

Working together would remind us that we were not alone and that we did not need to carry the load by ourselves. Haggai said God will bless us. Maybe those good things would be the way God would bless us.

After much hard work by Haggai and many people, the temple foundation was ready. The job was not finished, but we could see the shape of a new building. This second temple felt like the start of a new time for our city. We were home, again.

EZRA NEHEMIAH

The one with us and them

WHO IS IN & WHO IS OUT

As told by Aaron Higashi

Once upon a time in the court of the Persian king, there lived a man called Ezra. Ezra was a scribe who loved and studied the teachings of Moses, and the king of Persia gave him all that he asked for because the LORD his God was with him. (With Ezra, not the king.) And what Ezra wanted—more than anything in the whole wide world—was to study Torah and to do it in Jerusalem.

Now the king of Persia thought Ezra was wonderful, so he allowed Ezra to leave Babylon and return to Jerusalem with his blessing, but he asked Ezra to keep an eye on things while he was there. So Ezra gathered up some families who were still living in exile and they prepared to return to a home that many of them had only heard of and never seen.

Can you imagine it?

Ezra, after years of praying and longing to go home, was finally setting off to worship at the newly rebuilt temple—the one Haggai encouraged the people to build—to live among God's people and follow God's laws. Just like everyone else! He would no longer be a stranger in a strange land.

Except, he was.

Because the Jerusalem of his imagination was not the Jerusalem he found when he arrived. For one thing, Judah was no longer called Judah—it was now known by the name the Persians called it, Yehud.

And for another thing, there were "the people of the land." The people of the land were those who stayed in Judah when others—like Ezra's family— were taken into exile. They loved God, so when the temple was being rebuilt, they offered to help. But the leadership in Jerusalem said no.

They decided that the "people of Israel" were only those people who had returned to Yehud from exile. And because the people of the land had stayed, well…on the land…instead of being sent into exile, as far as the leaders in Jerusalem were concerned, they weren't part of the "true" people of Israel.

The people of the land became bitter because their help was rejected and they did everything they could to prevent the temple from being rebuilt.

Despite this, the returning exiles put their trust in God through the prophets Haggai and Zechariah, and one by one, the obstacles to rebuilding the temple were dealt with. The temple was rebuilt and the walls of the city were restored. Now the people of Israel could worship God the way their ancestors had.

Except, they didn't, which is what Ezra found when he arrived.

So Ezra got up on a high wooden platform and read the Torah aloud for the whole community. (Since many of the books in the Bible hadn't been written yet, or hadn't been collected together, the Torah was the people's scripture.)

Ezra was an expert in the Torah, and under his leadership, the people of Israel became known for their study and use of scripture. But even in ancient times, scripture could be difficult to interpret.

Some of the officials in Jerusalem came to Ezra to complain that the people of Israel had married "foreigners" and the "people of the land." Now the Torah warned the people of Israel against marrying anyone who was not Israelite because those marriages might lead the people to worship other gods. But the Torah also tells stories about the people of Israel happily marrying other people without any problem at all.

Ezra had to decide which stories to apply to the situation in Jerusalem. Ezra prayed about what he should do, but God didn't give him a direct answer. The hard decision fell to him: Was he going to go with the stories in the Torah that allowed Israelites to marry other people? Or was he going to go with the stories in the Torah that warned against marrying other people? Out of fear and caution, Ezra chose to follow the stories that warned against marrying other people.

Ezra gathered all of the people and told the men that if they had married foreign women or people of the land, they had to divorce them. More than one hundred men divorced their wives and sent them—and their children— away. But as you should now expect from the Bible, some storytellers did not agree with Ezra…

The one with Ruth and Naomi

THE FAITHFUL FOREIGN WOMAN

As told by Havilah Dharamraj

Ruth looked back for the last time. Her hometown was already a blur in the distance. Before her lay the road to Bethlehem. Bethlehem, a strange city in the foreign land of Judah. Her new home.

And if a new home wasn't scary enough, Ruth was from Moab and Moabites were not welcome in the land of Judah. They even had a law that banned Moabites from worshipping with them, right up to the tenth generation! But here she was, with her mind made up to go live in Bethlehem for the rest of her life.

Ruth had a good reason for moving to Bethlehem and that reason was trudging along beside her: her mother-in-law, Naomi. Naomi was from Bethlehem. More than ten years ago, she had come to Moab to escape a terrible famine—she and her husband, and her two sons. Ruth had married one of those sons. But then, stuff happened. Bad stuff.

First, Naomi's husband died. Then her sons died, one after the other. Now, with all her men dead, sad and tired Naomi made a plan to return to her people. Back to Bethlehem, all by herself, with no hope for the future.

But Ruth wouldn't let her go alone. "I'll come with you," she said.

"You?" exclaimed Naomi, astonished. "What would you do in Bethlehem?"

"Be with you, of course!" Ruth replied. "I've come to love you, mama-in-law. I love you so much that I will go with you, look after you, and live with you."

"You mean, for always?" Naomi asked, hardly believing her ears. "Wouldn't you be better off with your family in Moab?"

"Your family is my family," Ruth said. "So your hometown will be my hometown. And when I'm old and die, I even want to be buried next to where you are buried!"

"What about God?" Naomi asked. "Don't you worship a different god?"

"Your God is now my God," declared Ruth. "And that's that! Let's go to Bethlehem."

When they arrived in Bethlehem, everybody got talking about them. "Naomi's brought a Moabite daughter-in-law with her!" some people said. They didn't think this was good at all.

But others said, "Ruth is a foreigner alright, but think how kind it was of her to come with old Naomi. Look how well she takes care of her! She shows such loyalty!"

"She does?" asked some people. "Of course she does!" said the others. "Just this morning, Ruth was out in the barley fields, gleaning."

Now gleaning was something very poor people did. When rich, land-owning people harvested their crops, they left the edges of the field uncut. And when they bundled the stalks of grain, they didn't pick up any that fell out. God gave the people this law of kindness to protect poor people—people like Ruth and Naomi. They could come along to pick up the generous leftover crops and the grain that they gleaned would feed them for a whole season.

Gleaning in the barley fields was how Ruth met Boaz. Boaz was a rich man who owned the field in which Ruth was working. He had heard all about Ruth and was super impressed at her loyalty towards Naomi. It made Boaz want to be kind to the foreigner. All through the harvest he welcomed Ruth to his fields and made sure she had plenty of grain to take home.

Ruth was happy that she and Naomi had enough to eat every day. But, what would happen once the harvest season was done? How would they manage?

Naomi made a plan. Boaz was her husband's relative. And God had given the people a law to protect widows—women whose husband had died—like Naomi and Ruth. This law said that the brother or uncle or cousin of the man who died should marry his widow and take care of her forever. So, Naomi asked Ruth to go and meet Boaz. Now Boaz was a bit older than

Ruth, but Ruth was sure that if she married Boaz, he would take really good care of old, sad Naomi.

Imagine how surprised Boaz was when Ruth asked him to marry her! Boaz gladly agreed. And everyone, just everyone, in Bethlehem came to the wedding. Ruth may have been a Moabite, but she was no longer a stranger. God helped her belong in a Bethlehem family.

The People of God

Ruth's story is part of a big conversation in the Bible about who the people of God were. And this conversation got really loud after the Babylonian exile. Now there were many groups of people who worshipped God, but not in the same place or in the same way.

So, who were the people of God?

There were some, like Ezra, who thought only those who had been exiled to Babylon and returned to Yehud (Judah) could be the people of God. They worried that allowing others into their community might change who they were and make them less faithful to God.

And there were some, like the storyteller of Ruth, who thought the people of God included anyone who loved God—even foreigners!—and demonstrated that love through loyalty, kindness, and justice.

And then there were some who were exiled but chose not to return to Yehud when the Persians said they could. Instead, they continued to live in their new homelands. This diaspora community—spread all over the world—found new ways to worship and be faithful to God, as we see in the story of Esther.

Though each of these storytellers answers this question differently, all of them have something to teach us about what it means to be the people of God.

ESTHER

The one where Esther saves her people

FOR SUCH A TIME AS THIS

As told by Monica J. Melanchthon

Ahasuerus, the king of Persia, was a little bit ridiculous. He loved hosting parties in his palace in Susa with lots of drinking and feasting that lasted many days. Now, this might not sound ridiculous, but here's the thing: Vashti, his queen, was beautiful, and Ahasuerus wanted to show her off. He ordered his servants to bring her before them wearing her royal robes and crown. But Vashti refused. She did not want to be paraded before a group of drunken men and this made the king very angry. He and his officials were afraid other women in the kingdom would copy Vashti and not obey their husbands. So, the king said Vashti could no longer be queen and he sent her away. See? Ridiculous!

As King Ahasuerus no longer had a queen, all of the beautiful unmarried girls in the kingdom were brought to the palace, so that he could choose a new queen. The young women were given beauty treatments for a whole year before they appeared before the king. They were not allowed to go home and they missed their families.

After the exile, there were many Jews living in Persia and Mordecai was one of them. Mordecai was raising his orphaned cousin, Hadassah, who was young and beautiful and unmarried. Hadassah was given the Persian name Esther, which means, "star," but in Hebrew sounded like "hiding," because she was—sort of. Young and beautiful Esther was one of the girls taken to the king's palace. While she was there, Mordecai told her not to tell anyone that she was a Jew; he hoped that her Persian name might keep her safe.

Each night in the palace, one young woman was taken to King Ahasuerus and he would spend time with her. When Esther's turn came, the king loved her more than all of the others and made her his new queen.

But Mordecai did not forget Esther. One day while at the king's gate, he heard two of the guards planning to kill the king. Mordecai sent a message to Esther, and Esther told the king what Mordecai had heard. The matter was investigated and found to be true. Mordecai and Queen Esther saved the king!

But the ridiculous king had an even more ridiculous chief advisor— Haman. The king had ordered everyone at the gate to bow to Haman, but Mordecai refused because Jews only bowed to God. This made Haman furious. His friends advised him to have Mordecai killed, but Haman plotted to kill all the Jews, not just Mordecai. See? Ridiculous!

He said to the king, "The Jews are different from us, and they disregard your rules. You should destroy them." The king permitted Haman to do what was necessary, so Haman sent a decree (which is an order from the king) to all of the town officials across the empire telling them to kill all the Jews on the thirteenth day in the month of Adar.

The Jews, hearing this, became afraid. They cried and fasted and prayed. Mordecai wore sackcloth, which is what people wore when they were mourning, and sent messages to Esther to tell her what was happening. "You can help us," he said. "Perhaps you became queen for such a time as this."

Esther knew she had to find a way to save her people. No one—not even the queen— was allowed to see the king unless they were called. You could be killed for doing so! But Esther was willing to take the risk. Luckily, the king was happy to see her. He told her she could ask for anything and it would be given to her. So Esther invited the king and Haman to a banquet. This might sound suprising, but it was all part of Esther's plan.

The king was so pleased at the banquet that he again told Queen Esther that she could ask for anything and it would be given to her. "Please spare my life and the lives of my people," Esther humbly said, "for we have been told that we are all going to be killed."

The king was surprised. "Who made this decision?" he asked.

Esther pointed to Haman. The king was shocked and angry. He ordered Haman's death and gave all of Haman's wealth to Esther. Mordecai was put in charge of Haman's estate.

Queen Esther then told the king that she was a Jew, and begged him to stop her people from being killed as Haman had planned. The trouble was no one—not even the king—could undo a king's decree. (Ridiculous!) So the king let Mordecai send out a new decree that instructed the Jews to destroy anyone who tried to harm them on the day that Haman had set for their destruction.

And they did. Many people died that day as a result of Haman's foolishness, but Esther had saved her people.

To this day, Esther's bravery is remembered on Purim, when Jewish people tell the story of a ridiculous king and a very clever queen, and send food and gifts to one another in celebration of the day they survived.

"Of Judah"

Not every family sent into exile chose to return to Judah when the Persian king allowed the people to return. Many families chose to stay in the places they had settled in during the exile, and some moved even further away.

They formed communities throughout the Persian empire, in Egypt, and beyond, and these communities became known as diaspora communities. (Diaspora is a Greek word that means "to scatter about.")

But though these diaspora communities were far from Jerusalem and the temple, the people continued to worship God, share their stories, and follow torah in their new lands. Over time, they found new ways to be faithful to God.

Some of these ways set them apart from their neighbors. For example, they kept the Sabbath holy, which meant keeping the seventh day of the week as a day for rest and worship, not work. And they did not eat pork (meat from pigs) and other foods that are unclean (not okay) under the law. And they refused to bow down to anyone but God, like Mordecai.

Mordecai and Esther's story is a diaspora story. It shows the people what faithfulness to God looks like when you live away from Jerusalem and Judah. Even so, the storytellers call Esther and Mordecai "yehudi" in Hebrew, which means "of Judah." In English, this is translated as "Jew."

The one about being faithful

IN THE LIONS' DEN

As told by Brian Fiu Kolia

Once upon a time, there was a terrible king who thought he was rather wonderful. So wonderful, in fact, that he called himself Epiphanes which means "the one who reveals God." But everyone else called him Epipanes which means "the madman." This king thought his hometown of Antioch was pretty wonderful too, and he wanted everywhere he ruled to be just like his hometown. One terrible day this horrible king came and attacked Jerusalem. He put statues of his gods in the temple and forced the priests who served God to ignore the way God wanted them to live because he wanted the people of God to be just like the people of his hometown. Luckily, the people remembered other kings from times long, long ago, who were a bit like this terrible king. More importantly, they remembered the stories of the people who resisted these kings, and one of these people was Daniel.

Long ago, Daniel was forced to leave his home in Judah. Daniel was one of the people who were taken into exile to the faraway land of Babylon, which was ruled at the time by a scary king named Nebuchadnezzar. Now Daniel had three friends and their names were Hananiah, Mishael, and Azariah. Just like the frightful King Epiphanes, Nebuchadnezzar wanted the people of Judah to ignore how God wanted them to act by worshipping a huge statue. But Hananiah, Mishael, and Azariah (who were given the names Shadrach, Meshach, and Abednego) refused to bow down to the huge statue. Instead, they worshipped God. As punishment, Nebuchadnezzar ordered the three friends to be thrown into a sweltering fire. (I told you he was scary!)

But to the shock and amazement of all who were there, when the friends were thrown into the fire none of them suffered burns, nor did they even smell of smoke! Eventually, they were released, and King Nebuchadnezzar admitted that the friends were, in fact, servants of the Most High God. And this amazing story leads to another wonderful tale of faithfulness.

****

The years passed and Daniel grew much older. The terrible King Nebuchadnezzar of Babylon no longer ruled over Judah. A new ruler and kingdom came into power, and this king was not as cruel as Nebuchadnezzar. The new king's name was Darius the Mede, and he was the king of Persia. King Darius was not one to make decisions by himself (as Nebuchadnezzar had done). He chose 120 governors to help look after the kingdom, and three leaders to oversee the 120 governors—one of those leaders was Daniel.

Darius really liked Daniel and planned to make him chief leader over the whole kingdom. But some of the other governors and officials didn't like this, so they came up with a plan to make sure Darius wouldn't promote Daniel. They couldn't find anything bad to say about Daniel, so instead, they decided to get King Darius to approve and sign a new law—a law that would trap Daniel! The law said that for thirty days everyone in the kingdom must pray only to Darius. (They knew Daniel could not do this—he would only pray to God.) Anyone who broke this law would be thrown into the king's den of lions.

Daniel knew of this law, but rather than hide in his room and pray to God, he opened his windows so that everyone could see him pray. And they did. The officials who created the law told King Darius about Daniel. This made King Darius really sad because he liked Daniel, but the law said he had to throw his friend Daniel inside the den with the hungry lions. (In those days, a law that was signed by the king could not be changed.)

So, King Darius gave the order and Daniel was thrown into the lions' den. Before they closed up the den with a rock, Darius called down to Daniel and said he hoped Daniel's God would save him. Darius went back to his palace, but for the whole night, he couldn't eat or sleep, because he was thinking about his friend Daniel.

The next morning, Darius ran to the den to see if Daniel was alive. He called out to Daniel, asking if Daniel's God had saved him. "Yes!" Daniel replied, "God sent an angel to close the mouths of the lions." Just like Daniel's friends had been saved from the fire, so too Daniel was saved from the lions because he was loyal to and trusted in God.

King Darius was filled with joy and had Daniel pulled up from the den. But the king was very angry at the officials who created the law to trap Daniel—he ordered that they and their families be thrown into the den of lions. (Which goes to show it's best not to upset even the not-so-scary ancient kings…) Then King Darius made another law, one that asked all the people of his kingdom to worship Daniel's God, who rescued him from the lions' den.

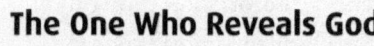

The One Who Reveals God

Around 200 years after the Persians defeated the Babylonians and took control of Jerusalem and Judah, there was a new emperor in town and this time it was a Greek one—Alexander the Great.

Alexander conquered huge areas of land—everything from Egypt to India—spreading his Greek language and culture throughout his new empire. When Alexander died, his generals fought for control of his lands, and Jerusalem and Judea (as it was now called) were right in the middle of them. Eventually Alexander's empire was divided between two generals: Ptolemy I in Eygpt and Seleucus I in Syria.

At first the Ptolemies in Egypt had influence in Judea, but eventually the Seleucids conquered the region. King Antiochus IV Epiphanes ("the one who reveals God") ruled the Seleucid empire from 175 BCE and he was the WORST. He took all of the gold and treasures from the Jerusalem temple, and he put statues of Greek gods in it. And he told the people that they were no longer allowed to follow God's torah.

Despite what he called himself, "Epiphanes" did not reveal God to the people. They had their stories for that. Daniel's story of faith and trust in God inspired the people to remain loyal to God, no matter what the terrible Epiphanes did.

2 MACCABEES

The one about resistance

EVEN MORE TROUBLE

As told by Shayna Sheinfeld

King Antiochus was not a very nice fellow. He was the ruler of a big kingdom called the Seleucid Empire. Inside his empire was the city of Jerusalem, and in Jerusalem was the Temple where Jews worshipped God. People called priests took care of running the Temple, and the main person in charge was called the High Priest, who was chosen in a special way. But King Antiochus decided that the best person to be High Priest of the Jerusalem Temple would actually be whoever paid him the most money.

This caused a lot of problems. Many people were unhappy with King Antiochus because they wanted the High Priest to be someone who loved God and who would take good care of the Temple. But the king didn't care. He just wanted lots of money.

Some priests didn't want the changes and others tried to pay Antiochus so they could be the High Priest. They started fighting each other, and some of them even brought armies into Jerusalem! But the king didn't know the priests were fighting each other. He thought the armies were coming to fight him.

So King Antiochus marched his own big army into Jerusalem. He decided to go into the Jewish Temple and steal or ruin all the special things that belonged to God. He also took all the money that was saved to keep the Temple running. And then (this is the worst part!) he said people should worship another god at the Jewish Temple, not the God of the Jews.

Not only that, King Antiochus said that Jews were not even allowed to be Jewish anymore. He did not let them do the things that God had said Jews should do, such as keeping kosher, which means only eating certain foods and not eating other foods. The king tried to force Jews to eat things that God said they shouldn't eat, like pork. And he did not let them keep the Sabbath or do other things that God said they should do.

Many Jews were very sad and angry. They had very big feelings about this. (Do you ever have big feelings about something that is important to you?) Some Jews decided they would do what God told them to do even if it was dangerous. And it was very dangerous!

King Antiochus tried to make an old man named Eleazar eat pork. The king said that Eleazar could either disobey God and eat the pork or he would be killed! Antiochus's soldiers felt bad for Eleazar because he was so old. They whispered to him to just pretend to eat the pork so that other Jews would be fooled into eating pork too.

Eleazar said "No! I will not even pretend to do something that God said not to do. I don't want other people to learn to do bad things because of me." So King Antiochus had him killed.

Next, the king tried to convince a mother and her seven children to eat pork. First, the oldest child refused to break God's commandment, so the king had him killed. One by one, each of the kids bravely stood up to the king, and each of them was killed while their mother had to watch. When only the youngest child was left, the mother told them to be brave and to follow God, and that God would take care of all of the people in this world or in the next world. So the youngest child stood up to the king and was killed too. Last of all, after watching her children act bravely to follow God's commandments, the mother was also killed.

If this story is making you sad, it's okay, because it's a sad story. And if it makes you mad, that is okay too. It made other people sad and mad also, including one Jewish man named Judah. They called him Maccabee as a nickname because it means "hammer." (Do you have a nickname?) Judah got this nickname because he was so sad and so mad that he decided to fight against King Antiochus. Like a hammer hitting a nail, Judah's fighting was focused and fierce. He gathered an army together and told King Antiochus and his army to leave them alone…or else! He said, "King! Let us worship God in the Temple and let us be Jewish the way we want to be!" The king did not listen. Judah Maccabee and his army had to fight a lot to get the king to leave them alone. They prayed to God and asked for God's help, and they won!

When Judah Maccabee and the Jews were able to get back into God's Temple, they saw what a BIG MESS the king and his soldiers had made. So they spent a long time cleaning it and putting everything where it belonged. It was a lot of work! Finally the Temple was ready for God. They were so happy to be able to worship God at the Jerusalem Temple again that they celebrated for eight whole days! Then the Jews decided that every year they would have a special holiday eight days long to remember this first time when they dedicated the Temple back to God. That holiday is called Hanukah, which means "dedication," and Jews today still celebrate it.

A-What-Crypha?

Did you know that different Bibles have different books in them? Well they do!

Jewish Bibles are made up of three parts: the Torah (the Teachings), the Nevi'im (the Prophets), and the Ketuvim (the Writings). Together, these are called the Tanak.

Christian Bibles include the same books as the Tanak, plus the books in the New Testament (the Gospels, Acts, and Letters).

But some Christian Bibles include even more books, and these are called the Apocrypha (or Deuterocanonical, "second canon") books. These were written between 200 BCE and 100 CE in many different places by many different people, but all of them can tell us something about

what life was like for Jewish people at this time.

Some of these books, like Maccabees 1 and 2, tell the stories of people who chose to remain faithful to God and God's laws in very difficult circumstances. Eleazar, and the mother and her seven sons, even died rather than betray God. They were called martyrs. Judah Maccabee's resistance led to a new set of kings in Judea—the Hasmoneans—who ruled until the Romans came in 63 BCE.

To this day, different Bibles have different books! But all of them can teach us something about the ancient world and the people who tell the Bible's stories.

The one where everything changes

ON THE ROAD TO DAMASCUS

As told by Sarah Emanuel

Saul grew up believing that a king would one day help the world. This king would not be like any other king. He would not rule over a small territory for a short amount of time. He would not stay home and feast while others fought his battles. Instead, this king would overthrow all of the world's evils and, with the help of God, establish a new world order where suffering would end and goodness would prevail forever.

Life was hard in the ancient world, but it was harder for some than others. Saul, a Jewish man from Tarsus, was just one of many Jews awaiting the arrival of this helper from God. His people even had a special name for this king: mashiach (which means "anointed") in Hebrew and christos in Greek. In English, we call this king "messiah."

But even though many Jewish people believed a messiah was coming, they sometimes disagreed about who the messiah would be. Saul probably heard all sorts of ideas shared in his local synagogue when he was a child.

"The messiah will be a super warrior!" Avraham might have said.

"The messiah will be a heavenly helper!" Miriam may have retorted.

"The messiah will be a great prophet!" Rivka might have countered.

Years later, when Saul was all grown up and living in Judea, he heard people saying that a man named Yeshua from Nazareth was the long-awaited messiah. In English, we call this man Jesus. Saul did not believe what people were saying about Jesus. In fact, he was so convinced these people were wrong, he yelled at them and fought them.

"Jesus is not our king!" Saul exclaimed. "Stop spreading lies!"

Saul had good reason not to believe. The Roman Empire, who many thought the messiah would overthrow, had killed Jesus. Saul could not see how Jesus, a man killed by enemy forces—a man who was dead!—could beat the Roman Empire, help people who were suffering, and bring peace. The messiah was supposed to end human pain. But pain remained.

"Jesus is not the one!" he shouted. "Don't you see we are still suffering? Don't you see the empire killed him?"

* * * * * * * * * *

One day, Saul was on his way to the nearby city of Damascus when he saw a light shine from heaven and flash all around him. He fell to the ground and heard a voice say, "Saul, Saul, why do you persecute me?"

Saul asked in reply, "Who are you, Lord?"

"I am Jesus," came the reply. "The one you are persecuting. Go into the city of Damascus and you will be told what to do."

When Saul got up, he realized he could no longer see. Even with his eyes wide open, he saw nothing. Luckily, Saul was not by himself. Some men traveling with him heard the voice too and helped Saul get to Damascus. For three whole days, Saul saw nothing.

Meanwhile, in Damascus there lived a believer of Jesus named Ananias. The Lord came to him in a vision. "Ananias," said the Lord. "Get up and look for a man from Tarsus named Saul. He is the one who will help spread the message of Jesus as the messiah."

At the same time, Saul also received a vision that Ananias would help him regain his sight.

So Ananias went to Saul, put his hands upon him, and said, "Brother Saul, the Lord Jesus, who appeared to you on your way here, has sent me so that you may regain your sight."

In that moment, something like scales fell from Saul's eyes. Ananias's healing remedy worked! Saul could see! Saul cleansed himself in a Jewish ritual bath, ate some food, and regained his strength. Imagine how relieved and thankful he must have been.

But it was not just strength that Saul gained that day—he also gained a new way of seeing things. For several days, Saul spent time with Jesus's students and messengers in Damascus, not as their opponent but as their friend. Saul began to believe that Jesus was indeed the messiah, just as the Lord told Ananias.

"Jesus is our messiah! He is going to help us!" Saul proclaimed from city to city.

Of course, not everyone believed Saul, but Saul was not discouraged. He continued to speak of Jesus to anyone who would listen—Jewish and non-Jewish people alike—for he thought everyone should learn of the good news he carried.

Waiting

Have you ever waited for something special? A birthday perhaps? Or a visit from a friend?

Waiting can be hard. But it can be even harder when what we are waiting for is something that we need.

Life in first-century Judea was hard. The empires of the past were a distant memory, but a mighty new empire now ruled over the lands: the Roman Empire.

The Romans were good at many things. They were good at building roads and buildings and water networks. They were good at creating laws and artworks and stories. And they were very good at telling people how good they were.

They had a phrase—Pax Romana—which means "Roman peace." This sounds good, and for some people it was. The Pax Romana was a time of wealth and peace for many. But the Pax Romana was a forced peace. For those who lived in the lands the Romans colonized—lands like Judea—this "peace" looked like soldiers, and taxes, and endless suffering.

And so the people watched and waited for a special helper from God who would save them and end their suffering.

Saul, who was also called Paul, waited, too. So you can understand why he wanted to tell everyone about Jesus! His letters are some of the oldest writings we have in the New Testament—even older than the Gospels.

The one where we remember Jesus

THE STORY COLLECTORS

As told by Isaac T. Soon

"It's been fifty Passovers since Jesus was raised from the dead. It's been decades since Paul and Peter passed on in Rome. And it's been almost ten years since the Romans destroyed the temple." Melissa's voice rose above the conversations around her. "We have collections of Jesus stories already," she continued. "We've heard the same tales. The same miracles! Why do we need one more?"

The talking and laughter in the rented hall quieted. The community was gathered together, as they were each week, to eat, sing, pray, and remember Jesus of Nazareth. All eyes turned to the corner of the room, where Melissa, a young enslaved girl, and her enslaver, known in the community as The Elder, were sitting on the floor among a pile of scrolls. Some were on the ground. Others were in a bag. Some were tied together. The Elder was reading each one aloud to anyone who wanted to listen.

At her question, he turned to Melissa with a smile. "Don't you know the wealth of riches at your feet? Do you think we have traveled across land and sea for months to gather stories we've already heard?"

He began shuffling through scrolls, reading the first line of each one until he found the one he was looking for.

"Listen to this," the Elder said. He read from a scroll, "The master Jesus, on the night he was handed over to be killed. He took bread, blessing it and breaking it, and said, "This is my body given on behalf of you. Do this in my memory."

All ears at the feast were now listening.

The Elder picked up another scroll. "But listen to this one: 'While they were eating, he took bread, blessed and broke it, and gave it to his disciples and said, "Take, this is my body."'—What do you notice?"

"It's the same," a little boy called out from among the crowd.

"No," said Melissa, her eyebrows bending into a furrow. "It's not the same. He says more in the one than in the other."

"Exactly," said The Elder. "Is one right and another wrong? Did someone make a mistake? Did he say both things? Did he say none of it? This is why we want a new collection of Jesus stories, double-checked and in order. To find out what really happened."

At that moment, someone handed The Elder a chunk of bread. Enslaved workers from each household began to hand out pieces of bread and cups of wine to everyone, before dividing the bread and wine among themselves. It was time to remember.

"Which passage should we read?" someone asked. Onlookers looked around and searched the crowd until their eyes fell on an elderly woman helping to pour wine into people's cups. Her name was Nympha, and she was the leader of this community. She paused and thought for a moment, then smiled and said, "Why not both?"

As The Elder read the scrolls aloud, a reverent silence fell upon the heads and hearts of all in the room.

When he had finished reading, and after every morsel of bread and sip of wine had been consumed, Melissa closed her eyes, lifted her arms up in the air, and raised her voice, blessing the meal with a traditional Jewish prayer: "Behold, this poor bread, which our Lord ate in the land of Israel. Let anyone who is hungry come in and eat. Let anyone who is in need come in and make peace."

As the glow of the embers faded, and the singing and chatter turned to dreams and gentle sighs, The Elder and Melissa opened up a blank scroll. Melissa finally understood why they had been traveling and collecting stories for so long.

As The Elder spoke softly, Melissa began to write:

"Although many have written down stories about Jesus, stories
that had been handed down to us from those who saw it for
themselves, I also decided to write everything in an orderly way to
you, Theophilus, so that you can stand steady in what you have
learned..."

Why Four Gospels?

The four Gospels in the New Testament were written decades after Jesus walked and taught in Galilee and Judea. In the early days of the church, those who walked alongside Jesus and learned from him told stories of who Jesus was and what he did. They told these stories to anyone who would listen, and stories of Jesus spread far and wide.

Eventually, the early storytellers died, but the stories they told lived on. Communities all over the place began to write these Jesus stories down and share them with other communities. Stories were swapped from person to person, with each community collecting and retelling the stories that best helped them understand who Jesus was and how they were meant to live.

This collection of stories looked different for each group of Jesus followers, which is why we have four collections of stories sharing the good news—or gospel—of Jesus in our Bibles. These Gospels don't always match and sometimes they disagree! But that's okay, because, like other ancient storytellers, the Gospel writers were less interested in preserving the minor factual details of Jesus's life and more interested in telling their readers the "big picture" story about who Jesus was.

LUKE 1:26–56

The one with hope for the oppressed

MARY'S SONG

As told by Jennifer Garcia Bashaw

"Greetings, favored one! The Lord is with you."

Mary jumped when she heard the words of the angel, startled by the strange greeting and the even stranger visitor who had come to her home in Nazareth.

"Do not be afraid," the angel Gabriel said to Mary, "God is going to bless you. You are going to have a baby and you will name him Jesus. He will be great and will be called the Son of God, and the Lord will give to him the throne of his ancestor David."

Mary's breathing sped up as doubts raced through her head. "How am I going to have a baby?" she thought. "And not just any baby, but a king—the son of God? I am not married. I am not royalty. I am a nobody from a nowhere town. This all seems impossible."

Mary voiced her questions out loud and the angel reassured her that the Spirit could help her with the details. Then he spoke words that took root inside her and would give her strength for years to come.

"Nothing will be impossible with God."

With this reassurance, Mary stood up confidently and answered the angel in the way of Israel's prophets before her: "Here am I, the servant of the Lord." She knew that the task God chose for her would be difficult, but she would face the challenges with faith and courage like the mothers of faith who came before her. (Can you remember some of their names and the challenges they faced?)

One challenge Mary faced was that her friends and neighbors might not have liked the idea of an unmarried woman having a baby, so Mary went to another town to stay with her relative, Elizabeth. Just like Mary, Elizabeth was going to have a baby.

As soon as Mary arrived at Elizabeth's home and called out to greet her, something amazing happened. Elizabeth's baby—who would later be called John the Baptist—jumped for joy inside her. Then, Elizabeth was filled with the Holy Spirit. Being filled with the Holy Spirit can mean many things, but here it meant that Elizabeth was about to speak on God's behalf.

"You are special, Mary," Elizabeth said, "and so is the baby you are going to have! You believed in God's promises and they will come true!"

Mary answered Elizabeth with her own prophecy, a song that painted a picture of who God is and how her baby was going to change the world.

My soul magnifies the Lord,
and my spirit rejoices in God my Savior,
You have done great things for me,
even though I feel so small and unimportant.

God, you have always been merciful and kind
To all who need your strength.
You have pulled the powerful people down
and lifted up the people who have no power at all;

You have fed the poor and hungry
and have sent the rich away empty.
You have helped your people Israel,
showing mercy and compassion,
You fulfilled the promise you made to us,
to Abraham, and to his family forever.

One day, Mary's baby, Jesus, would grow up and teach the same things that Mary preached that day—that the kin-dom of God is not like any kingdom in the world. Human kingdoms value people with money and privilege and power. But God's kin-dom values the poor, the people without power, and those who have been harmed and ignored by the people in charge. The kin-dom that Jesus teaches is more like a family—a family that turns the world upside down.

The World of the Gospels

Jesus probably lived from around 4 BCE to 30 CE, but the Gospels were written many years later, and lots had changed by then.

People who study the Bible believe that Mark's Gospel (likely the first Gospel to be written) was written during a time of great suffering, sometime around 65–70 CE.

This was a tough time for Jewish people living in Judea. Their attempts to free themselves from the Roman Empire were met with violence from Roman armies. In 70 CE, Rome sacked the city of Jerusalem and the temple was destroyed...again.

The Gospels of Matthew and Luke were likely written 15 to 20 years after this, and the Gospel According to John even later.

Those following Jesus looked different, too. Thanks to Saul's (Paul's) amazing efforts sharing the news of Jesus, the number of Jesus followers had grown and now included a lot of non-Jewish people. This made things tricky, as people tried to work out what was (and was not) required of Jesus's followers. Did they have to follow torah, for example, or was faith in Jesus enough?

The Gospel writers had all of these things in mind when they wrote their Gospels, so their stories often reflect two worlds: the world Jesus lived in and the world they lived in.

Mary's song showed Luke's readers, who perhaps did not know torah and the prophets, what God's kin-dom was like and how they were meant to live.

The one where God is with us

WELCOME, BABY JESUS

As told by Shannon K. Evans

Joseph was in shock. Mary had told him what the angel said, but it sounded impossible. How could he believe it? He went to sleep that night feeling overwhelmed and confused.

As he slept, an angel came to him in a dream, saying, "Do not be afraid, Joseph. Believe her. The baby inside Mary really is from the Holy Spirit, and when he's born you are to name him Jesus." Joseph woke up and knew what to do. They would be a family.

Not long after, so the story goes, the Roman Emperor Caesar Augustus declared that everyone in the Roman Empire must be counted in a census, and each family must return to their hometown to register. Joseph and Mary were living in Nazareth, but Joseph's family was from Bethlehem, so to be counted they would have to make a journey.

When they arrived in Bethlehem, the town was packed with people. All of the guest rooms were full, so Mary and Joseph were given shelter in a family room, where the farm animals slept.

Soon, it was time for Mary to have her baby. Joseph, perhaps helped by the women of the home they were staying in, made the space clean and comfortable. When Mary birthed Jesus into the world, a sacred feeling came upon the room.

"Emmanuel," she whispered. *"God is with us."*

Mary swaddled Jesus in blankets and kissed his nose. When he cried, she fed him her milk. When he pooped, she changed his wraps. When he fell asleep, she handed him to Joseph, who paced back and forth with the baby in his arms, humming softly.

"Emmanuel," Joseph sang. *"God is with us."*

Then Joseph laid baby Jesus down in the manger, and the new parents closed their eyes for some well-deserved rest.

What Mary and Joseph did not know was that as they slept, angels had appeared above a nearby field, where shepherds were watching over their sheep. These shepherds were not rich or powerful, not particularly important, and probably a little stinky. (Sorry, but it's true.) But they got to be the first to hear about Jesus, because God doesn't care about that stuff.

"Don't be afraid," the angels said. "We have good news for all people! Today in Bethlehem the Messiah has been born! Go, find him; he'll be lying in a manger."

Then they sang:

Glory to God and peace on earth.

When the angels left, the shepherds looked at each other with their mouths hanging open. What just happened?! Would they really find a baby lying in a manger in Bethlehem?

Sure enough, they did find him—right where the angels said he would be. The shepherds relayed their story then returned home, praying and laughing and telling everyone what God had done. Mary marveled at yet another wonder, treasuring them in her heart. But the wonders weren't done yet.

Some time later, a group of magi (or as you may know them, "wise men") were traveling from the East. The magi spent their lives studying the stars, and had followed one particular star that represented the birth of the king of the Jews all the way to Jerusalem, the City of David.

"We've come to worship him," the magi told King Herod when they arrived in Jerusalem. But Herod was perplexed. After all, he was the king! So he gathered his priests and teachers and asked them where the Messiah was prophesied to be born.

"Oh, that's easy," they all agreed. "In Bethlehem."

Herod worried that this baby would grow up to take his throne. He couldn't have that. He would have to be sneaky. Herod said to the magi, "Go on to Bethlehem. And when you find the child, report to me, so that I too can worship."

But the magi were warned in a dream not to trust Herod. So when they left Jerusalem, they had no plans to come back. They would return home by a different route.

The magi followed the star until it stopped over the house Jesus was in. They were overjoyed, and presented him with gifts of gold, frankincense, and myrrh. (Yes, kids would rather get toys, but Mary probably appreciated these more.)

The shepherds, magi, Mary, and Joseph—they all knew there would be no returning to life as normal after this. The world would never be the same.

Emmanuel, God is with us.

Birth Stories

Have you heard the story of when you were born? Did you cry out when the cold air first touched your skin? Who gave you your first cuddle?

In the ancient world, birth stories were very important. They told us more than just what happened when a baby came into the world, they told us what kind of person that baby would be.

Take Moses, for example. He was placed in a basket in a river as a baby, just like a famous ancient king called Sargon. Moses's birth story showed the ancient Israelites that he was someone special—a great leader.

The Gospels of Mark and John don't have anything to say about the birth of Jesus,

but the Gospels of Matthew and Luke do. In Luke's Gospel, angels appear to shepherds in a field. In Luke's birth story, God wants the poor and stinky shepherds to know that Jesus has been born because Luke wanted people to know that Jesus cared deeply for the poor.

In Matthew's Gospel, magi travel a great distance to worship "the king of the Jews". Matthew wanted to be sure his readers—like the magi—could see the difference between Rome's leaders and God's long-awaited messiah.

Though very different, both Luke and Matthew's birth stories show us something important their writers wanted us to know about Jesus.

The one with John the Baptist

LEADING THE WAY

As told by Tamice Spencer-Helms

John the Baptist had a secret. John was aware of something so big that it changed everything about how he interacted with the world.

This secret made him live in a way that was very different from everyone else. He lived out in the boonies, and people made fun of what he ate and how he dressed, but he knew something they didn't know…

Before he was born, God said John was going to be important—someone who would make a big difference in the world. And he was related to Jesus, who was his cousin! That's right, when John and Jesus were together, everyone could feel that something special was happening.

Both John and his cousin Jesus followed their callings in their own unique ways. The things they did were so unexpected and groundbreaking that they surprised everyone around them.

Just like Jesus, John's birth story was pretty special. John's mother Elizabeth was very old when she had John, which was a miracle all by itself. And one day his dad Zechariah met an angel at the temple who said John would be part of a big, heavenly plan. But unlike Jesus's mother Mary, Zechariah did not believe the angel, so he wasn't able to speak at all while Elizabeth was pregnant with John.

Now John's parents were pretty well-known and respected. They had a lot of stuff and were considered important. Sometimes having a lot to lose can make us feel pressure not to rock the boat. But for John, it meant something altogether different. He saw that things in the world could be better and he chose to show that by living differently.

John lived in the wilderness, where people like him didn't normally live, and he ate things like locusts, that people who come from families like his didn't normally eat.

He left all the fancy things behind and decided to be true to himself. That's a tough thing to do, especially when other people might not get it. They might think you're strange or make fun of you. But John knew that being true to what you believe is super important. It's okay to be different if you're doing what you feel is right.

Jesus chose his own unique path, too. When he was just twelve years old, his family headed home from a visit to Jerusalem, but Jesus stayed behind in the temple. Everyone was worried when they could not find him, but Jesus wasn't—he knew where he was the whole time.

While he was living in the wilderness, John became famous for his baptisms. He helped people begin anew and follow God more deeply. It's like he was giving them a fresh start, a do-over. This wasn't always easy for people to understand, but baptism was a powerful symbol. When John lowered people into the water, then lifted them up again, it was like they were being born again into a new life—a life where they could be brave, honest, and true to themselves. It was the beginning of something new and wonderful, like water breaking when a baby is born.

John even got to baptize his cousin Jesus to show what a "born again" life might look like. People were surprised by how John and Jesus chose to respond to the secret knowing they had—the knowledge that they were special to God and to the world. And surprises can be scary for some people. We often feel safer with things we know than with things we don't.

But John and Jesus, they were courageous and truthful, even when it meant standing up to powerful people who didn't like what they were saying. They were pioneers, leading the way to a world with less fear and more understanding.

John's message is especially powerful. He showed us that being authentic and standing up for what's right is important, even when it's hard or it makes you stand out. John's way of living—his choice to be in the wilderness and his baptisms—were how he showed his belief in a fresh start, a new way of living that was honest and true. He didn't just talk about change; he lived it. That's the kind of life that can really change the world, just like John the Baptist and Jesus did.

Disciples

Many respected teachers in the ancient world had disciples. We often think of disciples as being students, but discipleship in the time of Jesus involved much more than simply studying or learning something.

Ancient disciples literally followed their teacher, imitating their lives and teachings. A good disciple did what their teacher did, lived how their teacher lived, and eventually became just like their teacher.

John the Baptist had disciples. Many people loved the example John set with his life, and they wanted to be just like him. Some even thought that John was the long-awaited messiah—God's chosen one.

Perhaps that is why the Gospel writers were so careful to tell their readers that John was not the messiah, but the one who was sent ahead of the messiah.

Jesus also had a great many disciples. People came from all over to hear him teach. But there were some he was particularly close to and he spent extra time teaching them—people like Mary, Martha, and Zacchaeus. Then there were "the twelve" disciples who traveled with Jesus and had special responsibilities when he died. These included his good friends Peter, John, and James.

Today, there are millions of disciples of Jesus, but now we call them Christians.

The one about living and loving well

THE SERMON ON THE MOUNT

As told by Shane Claiborne

———————

After he was baptized by his cousin John, Jesus began to teach in synagogues and heal people and preach the good news of the kingdom of God. Word got around and people began to follow Jesus. Some of them left everything to become his disciples.

One day, there were so many people around Jesus that he climbed up on the side of a mountain to teach them. Kind of like Moses did long ago. Jesus taught the people many things that day, and began by blessing the most unlikely people…

****

Blessed are the poor in spirit…in God's family you belong because of who you are.

Blessed are those who are sad sometimes, because God loves to comfort people.

Blessed are the meek, the people who are shy sometimes, the ones who are not always the loudest or the strongest. In God's world, there is room for everybody, and those who get overlooked are given special attention.

Blessed are those who know what it feels like to be hungry, because they understand how good food really is.

Blessed are those who are full of mercy and love and compassion, who care for people, and who show kindness to people.

Blessed are the pure in heart—those who choose to love, over and over, even the people it is hard to like.

Blessed are the peacemakers—the people who don't like fighting, who can't stand to see someone get bullied or made fun of, who stick up for others, and who know that even bullies can learn how to be a friend if someone shows them.

Blessed are those who aren't popular—who people say mean things about or tell lies about. Don't worry, God knows the truth. And remember, even some of the greatest prophets were treated really badly, too.

You are like brown sugar on oatmeal. Or like rainbow sprinkles on ice cream. Or like chocolate syrup in milk. You can make the world a better place—you can live in a way that makes the world sweeter, more beautiful, more fun, more kind. Just like a flashlight or a candle can light up even the darkest room, that's what you are to be in this world—lights in the darkness.

Sometimes when people talk about the law or the prophets, it can feel like a lot of rules, but that's why I came—to help you understand. The rules are good! But, I want you to see what the rules are all about—they teach us how to love God and each other. All the rules are meant to protect us, and to keep us from hurting each other. They are meant to help us love better. Sometimes we miss the whole point of them, and that's why I came—to show you what perfect love looks like.

We all know it is wrong to kill someone. But it is also wrong to hate someone. It is wrong to call someone stupid. When we allow our hearts to grow hard and hate another person, we open the door to all sorts of bad things. Hate hurts the one who hates.

When you do something wrong, do what you can to make it right. When someone wrongs you, give them a chance to make it right. Work things out in a loving way.

If someone slaps you, don't slap them back, otherwise you are acting just like them. If they slap you, look them in the eyes, and let them know that they may have hurt your body, but they cannot hurt your soul. Your love is stronger than their meanness.

If someone tries to take your jacket, give them your gloves too. If someone sues you for your outer garment, give them your underwear! You are more than your possessions. No one can rob you of the things that really matter. Don't give mean people the power to control you or make you hate them.

If someone wants you to run an errand with them, even if you don't feel like it, run a few errands with them. You might be surprised at how generosity pays off and how contagious love is. So give generously. Err on the side of grace rather than greed.

You have heard it said, "Love your neighbor and hate your enemy." But I tell you love everybody, even your enemies. And pray for those who are mean to you. It's easy to only love our friends and family who love us back. Everybody does that. But you are to love as big as God loves. Love everybody, no exceptions.

Matthew

We don't actually know who wrote the Gospels as their writers never tell us their names. Since the second century though, people have said the Gospel According to Matthew was written by a disciple of Jesus called Matthew.

But there are some hints in the text that suggest this is unlikely. Some phrases, such as, "And this story is still told among the Jews to this day," make us think it was written years after Jesus lived, maybe as many as 50 or 60 years.

So we can't know for sure who wrote the Gospel of Matthew, but we'll call him Matthew to keep things simple.

Here's what we can guess though: Matthew was probably Jewish (like Jesus) and he believed Jesus was the long-awaited messiah. He knew the Torah and the Prophets well, and he wanted to show his readers how Jesus was connected to them. The Sermon on the Mount is a great example of this. This story is told in Luke's Gospel too, but there Jesus taught on a plain, not on a mountain. Matthew wanted to be sure his readers connected Jesus with Moses and his teachings with the Torah, so he made sure Jesus "looked" like Moses by saying he was on a mountain. And maybe he was!

Matthew's Gospel was probably written for a community with some new non-Jewish believers in Jesus, who probably lived a long way away from the lands in which Jesus lived and taught.

JOHN 9

The one where the man born blind sees

SEEING JESUS

As told by Elizabeth Enns Petters

———————

Jesus and his disciples were taking a walk along the roads of Jerusalem. As they were walking and talking, they passed a man who had been born blind, sitting alone.

The disciples asked Jesus whose fault it was that the man was born blind. (Jesus's friends sound a bit like Job's friends here, don't they?)

"You're asking the wrong question," Jesus replied. "You are looking for someone to blame…Look instead at what God can do."

Then Jesus did something a little odd. He knelt down next to the man, spit in the dirt, and started making mud pies. Just kidding. But he did spit in the dirt and then used his hands to make a thick paste that he spread over the eyes of the man born blind. Sounds a little gross doesn't it? A lot of people believe that saliva has healing properties, but just for small things like cuts and scrapes. This was a much bigger healing job.

After the paste was all over the man's eyes, Jesus told him to go wash it off in the nearby pool of Siloam. When he was all clean, the man realized he could see! I wonder how he felt? He was probably surprised and maybe a little overwhelmed.

Word traveled fast about the man who was healed. It was exciting and surprising, and people weren't sure if the man who was healed was the same man they had seen blind and begging, but he assured them, "It's me."

The thing is, it's not every day that someone gets healed, and some people still weren't sure about what had happened. So they went to the Pharisees, who studied *torah* and the prophets. The Pharisees thought very carefully about how they could honor the scriptures and their traditions in their daily lives.

When the Pharisees heard about Jesus and the man he had healed, they were concerned. It was the Sabbath—the day of rest—and people were meant to honor God by not working on this day. Healing looked like it might be work, so they had some questions. They decided to speak with the healed man himself.

The man told them about Jesus and the mud and the spit and the washing in the pool. He told them that he could see!

"What do you think about this Jesus guy?" the Pharisees asked him.

"He is a prophet," the man replied.

The Pharisees still weren't sure. Saying that someone is a prophet was a big deal. They wanted more information and so they found the parents of the man who was healed.

His parents told the Pharisees, "We know he is our son, and we know he was born blind. But we don't know who opened his eyes. Why don't you ask our son? He's a grown man and can speak for himself."

Clearly the Pharisees didn't get the information they wanted from the parents, so they went back to the man himself. This is starting to feel like a ping pong match, isn't it? Back and forth and back and forth.

The Pharisees really couldn't imagine anyone being able to heal another person, so they asked the man again what had happened.

The man who was healed said, "I was blind...I now see." End of story, right? Not quite.

"How did he open your eyes?" the Pharisees asked.

The man was getting a bit frustrated now and said, "I have told you over and over and you would not listen. Why do you want to hear it again? This guy healed me. He has to be connected to God in a special way or he would not have been able to do that."

The Pharisees did not like this answer, so they sent the man away from them. But guess who went to find him? Yup—Jesus!

"Do you believe in the Son of Man?" Jesus asked him. (Which is just a fancy way of asking if he believed in the long-awaited messiah.) The man looked around a bit and then said, "Point him out to me, sir." (Sometimes it can be really hard to believe things that seem impossible.)

Jesus understood this. "You're looking right at him," he said. And the man who was healed immediately replied, "I believe."

Then Jesus said, "Those who were blind, now see. But those who think they see, well...they do not see at all."

John

Did the answer the man's parents gave to the Pharisees seem a little rude to you? John says they were afraid they would be put out of the synagogue if they said Jesus was the messiah, and that is why they answered that way. This seems unlikely, though—that kind of thing didn't really happen when Jesus was alive, but perhaps it reflects tensions at the time John's Gospel was written.

As you probably remember, we don't know the real name of the person(s) who wrote the Gospel According to John, but we'll call them John anyway.

John is VERY different from the other three Gospels. Maybe this is because John heard different stories about Jesus. But maybe it's because of when this Gospel was written.

John's Gospel was probably written toward the end of the first century, when questions of identity and life under empire were once again a focus for Jewish people.

In the years after the First Jewish Revolt (66-70 CE), during which the temple was destroyed and Jewish resistance to Roman rule was brutally suppressed, synagogues rose in importance as local centers of worship. And those Jesus followers? Well, some of what they said and did could be a bit dangerous. The parents in this story might have been a reminder to John's readers to be bold and not be afraid to speak of Jesus.

MARK 2:1-12

The one where Jesus shows his authority

THROUGH THE ROOF

As told by Kylie Crabbe

───────────

As Jesus was gathering friends and followers, talking about the best ways to live and meeting all different kinds of people—many of whom were sad, or confused, or hurting—he sometimes annoyed some people or got them angry.

Often the people he angered were the leaders in his own religious community. They were worried about the kinds of things he was saying and doing. How was he so sure what God wanted?

Just like all through the Bible and right up to today, people questioned and disagreed with one another as they talked about how to follow God well and live faithfully.

The disagreements we see in the Gospels were about a whole lot of topics, like whether it was ok to do things—like heal people, or pick food to eat—on the Sabbath day of rest. Sometimes there were questions about who Jesus ate meals with. People who study the Bible call these stories "controversy stories," because in them there is a disagreement between Jesus and others about what it means to live lives faithful to God and God's laws.

In this story there is a controversy. See if you can find it…The story begins with Jesus at home in Capernaum. We don't usually imagine Jesus being at home, because most of the time when the Gospel writers tell us the things that Jesus did, they say he's traveling in villages or the countryside or by the sea, meeting people wherever they are. But as this story opens, Mark says word has gotten out to the crowds that Jesus is at home.

Jesus's quiet few days come to a quick end. People come flocking to him. They crowd out the house. You can't even get to the door! Jesus is preaching and everyone wants to hear what he's saying.

Four people arrive carrying a child on a bed. We do not know much about the child. We do not know their name, or age, or what they liked to eat, or what color hair they had. We know only that Jesus calls them "child" and that they are paralyzed and could not walk.

This made things tricky—the house is impossible for them to get into because of the crowd. Maybe the four people carrying the bed are the child's friends, or maybe they are enslaved servants who help the child get around. Either way, they are so very keen to get this child to Jesus that they carry the child up the outside stairs to the roof, dig a hole through the roof, and lower the child into the house right in front of Jesus!

Can you imagine?! What might Jesus have thought about having this happen to his roof? Well, he doesn't get mad, as you might expect someone would if people dug a giant hole in their roof. No, the first thing we're told is that Jesus notices "their" faith (not just one person's faith, but the faith of the friends).

And seeing this, Jesus says, "Child, your sins are forgiven." Of course, no one has actually asked Jesus to do any particular thing. He notices faith and responds by forgiving sin. None of this has anything to do with the child's paralysis—Jesus knows that anyone can have things they regret or wish they'd done differently that might weigh on them and make them feel bad, and he says all that is forgiven! You can let go of it!

It does get a cross response, though!

Some of the leaders in Jesus's community are there. They don't speak up, but Jesus knows that they're cross in their hearts. They think only God can forgive sins and they grumble that Jesus is doing the wrong thing, speaking in a way that only God should.

Of course, forgiving sins isn't a very visual thing. How would people inside that overcrowded house even know that it had happened, apart from Jesus saying it did?

So, as he responds to those leaders' worries, Jesus does something that will be visible to all—he tells the child to gather up the bed and walk home. And the child does!

This doesn't mean that healing was the same as forgiving sin, and it definitely doesn't mean that having a disability is the result of sin. Instead,

Jesus is pointing out that he has authority both to forgive sins (which he had already done, though it didn't have a very obvious visual effect), and to heal (which he also does, and this time it's an action that is visible to others).

The crowd is amazed! And all the crowd—including those who had been crossly questioning Jesus's authority in their hearts—glorify God, saying, "We never saw anything like this!"

Healing Stories

Many people lived with disability or illness in ancient times—everyone had differences, and they mostly just got on with life.

But there were some differences—like certain kinds of skin conditions—that some communities might have seen as a reason to exclude people. This reminds us that how we understand what disability is (or is not) can change across different times, places, and cultures.

Some of the biblical texts talk about whether sin can cause illness or disability. (Sin means to do something that goes against God or God's laws.) In the story of the man born blind, Jesus says no, this man's blindness is definitely not because of sin—not the man's sin, or his parents' sin, or anyone else's sin.

With so many healing stories in the Bible, it can look like the Bible is saying people with disabilities need to change in order to be a part of the community of faith. Or that if you are not healed, then you don't have enough faith. This is not true. Not all biblical stories about people with disabilities suggest healing or change is needed. As you read on in this book, you'll find a story Jesus tells about God's kingdom. In it, Jesus talks about how God's kingdom is like a big party where guests with disabilities are all welcomed, just as they are.

The one where Jesus restores

GET UP!

As told by Summer Kinard

Jairus's daughter would not wake up. His wife swayed on her feet as he walked into the room where she had kept another night's vigil by their girl.

"She didn't eat?" he asked.

His wife shook her head as she moved the tray of broth and water to a table. "I couldn't wake her. Jairus, she always wakes for me. What will we do?"

"I will go and get Jesus."

As he rushed out the door, he tried to breathe down his panic. Ever since their daughter had been born nearly twelve years ago, she had been the center of their lives. There was God, and Jairus's wife, and Jairus's daughter. Mornings were for praying—his chants waking the women—and watching his wife's practiced movements as she woke and fed their daughter. "Good morning, my daughter. Get up, little girl. It's time to eat." Every morning had been the same. "Get up, little girl. It's time to eat."

But these past few days had been a nightmare. Their daughter would not wake. She would not eat. His wife had dripped broth into the girl's mouth one drop at a time, but it had no effect. The fever would not lift. The girl would not wake.

Jairus saw a crowd in the street and ran to the Teacher, Jesus. He threw himself at Jesus's feet. "My daughter, my only daughter, is dying. Please come."

Jesus went with him, pressed on every side by the crowd.

They were on their way when suddenly, a woman approached who had not been able to attend synagogue much for twelve years. Her constant bleeding often made her too exhausted to stand for long, but Jairus recognized her as someone whose face lit up when she was able to attend.

He watched, stunned, as the woman came up behind Jesus in the crowd and stooped to touch his hem. Suddenly power came into her, like the glory of the temple and the smell of clean skin and the soft hands of children. Warmth filled her and the bleeding stopped. Her strength returned. Life and health flowed into her.

The teacher stopped walking. "Who touched me?" he asked.

His disciples and Jairus looked from Jesus to the crowd. "It wasn't us," they said.

The crowd shrugged.

Peter, one of the disciples, said, "Master, the multitudes surround you and press upon you!"

But Jesus said, "Someone touched me, for I felt the power leave me."

The woman had grown used to hiding, but at that moment she realized that she was no longer hidden. She fell down before Jesus and told him everything.

"Daughter," Jesus said, "Your faith has made you well; go in peace."

Jairus watched with gratitude that soon turned into fear. The woman had sought Jesus with her whole heart, and her faith was her path to healing. What of his own daughter, who could not speak or ask for help? Would there be a way for her to be healed as well?

Before Jesus finished speaking to the healed woman, a messenger came to Jairus. "Your daughter is dead. Do not trouble the Teacher."

But on hearing this Jesus answered him, "Do not fear; only believe, and she shall be well."

Jairus allowed himself to be led back toward his home. He had led the people in prayer a thousand times, ten thousand, maybe. But he had never seen anything like this. What doctor would try to heal the dead?

Jairus stumbled as they reached his home, where the keening women and sobbing men had already taken up their stations. He followed Jesus like a lamb into the room where his daughter had not woken up. He held his wife's hand and looked to the Teacher.

Jesus took the girl's hand and said, "Get up, little girl," the same way her parents woke her every morning.

The little girl woke and sat up in bed, drawing a long, long breath. "Give her something to eat," the Teacher said as he gave her to her parents.

Jairus's wife kissed the girl's face, and Jairus embraced them both. A servant ran to get the finest bread. The girl's parents were too overcome with gratitude and joy to speak. Jesus told them to tell no one what had happened.

JOHN 4

The one with the Samaritan woman

BY A WELL

As told by Jennifer T. Kaalund

One day when Jesus was on his way back to Galilee with his disciples, he stops in the Samaritan city of Sychar. Jesus is tired from the long journey, so his disciples go to get some food while Jesus rests by Jacob's well. Jacob's well was important to the Samaritans. Their ancestor, Jacob, dug this well so that they could have water. You remember Jacob? He's the one who wrestled with the stranger and had twelve sons, as well as daughters.

It was noon and a woman came to Jacob's well to get water. She was a Samaritan, but we do not know her name.

Jesus asks the woman for some water.

The woman is surprised by his request! It was strange for a man to talk to a woman he did not know.

Why is Jesus asking for water when he does not even have a bucket, she wondered?

So she asks him, "How is it that you, a Jew, ask a drink of me, a woman of Samaria?"

The woman points out all the ways they are different with her question.

"If only you knew who you were talking to," Jesus responds, "you would know that I can offer you something better than this refreshing well water." Then Jesus tells the Samaritan woman about another kind of water—living water.

"Where will you get this living water?" The woman challenges him. "Are you bigger and better than our ancestor Jacob?"

Jesus says living water is water that you can drink, and you will never be thirsty again.

The woman is intrigued by this living water that Jesus is talking about. This would mean never having to come back to the well to draw water again! So, she asks Jesus where she can find this living water.

Then Jesus does something really weird. He tells the Samaritan woman to go and get her husband and come back to the well.

The woman responds, "I do not have a husband." Jesus says, "You are right. You do not have a husband now, but you have been married five times."

She again is surprised. How does Jesus know these personal things about her? They have never met. She responds, "Sir, I see that you are a prophet. Our ancestors worshipped on this mountain, but your people worship in Jerusalem."

This time the woman is reminding Jesus of the different ways that Samaritans and Jewish people worship.

Jesus tells her that it doesn't matter if you worship God on the mountain or in the city, what matters is that you worship God honestly and with your whole heart. God is spirit. These differences don't matter to God.

(This might be a good time to mention that this story of Jesus and the Samaritan woman is only in the Gospel of John. John was probably writing for two groups of people who followed Jesus, but had different understandings of what that following should look like, so it was important to him that they hear this message.)

Then Jesus tells this smart woman who was willing to ask him difficult questions that he is the messiah, the one the people have been waiting for.

While Jesus and the woman are talking, the disciples return and they are shocked to find Jesus talking to a woman, but not just any woman—a Samaritan woman!

The woman leaves her jar of water at the well and runs into the city to tell everyone that she met a man who told her everything that she had ever done. She tells them that he indeed is a prophet, and she wonders if he may even be the long-awaited messiah.

Even though we do not know her name, this Samaritan woman must have been known in the city because the people hear her story and believe her!

Meanwhile the disciples were trying to convince Jesus to eat. Just as Jesus taught the woman about a different kind of water, he teaches the disciples about a different kind of food. Jesus describes food as doing the will of God—God who sent him to complete a task.

Like the living water satisfies thirst, doing God's will satisfies Jesus: it makes him feel full and whole, just like eating food and drinking water. We need food and water to take care of our bodies. We also need to take care of our spirits.

Many Samaritans believed in Jesus because of this woman's story. Jesus stays in Sychar for two more days and the people learn even more about God. Now they believe because of what they have learned. They say, ' Truly he is the savior of the world.'"

Who are the Samaritans?

If the word Samaritan sounds familiar it is probably because you have heard the parable or perhaps the term "the good Samaritan." Today a good Samaritan is someone who helps a stranger.

However, in the time of Jesus, Jews and the Samaritans did not get along. The Samaritans lived in Samaria, which was located in part of the area that used to be known as the northern kingdom of Israel, but had the name Samaria in Jesus's day.

The Samaritans might be the great-, great-, great-, great-, great- grandkids of Israelites who survived the Assyrian conquest, or they might be descended from the people who moved into the lands after the Assyrians swept through.

Either way, they share some similiar beliefs with the Jews, but there are some important differences. For example, both communities share stories of Jacob, who is mentioned in this story as an example of a shared ancestor.

But after the exile, the Samaritans built their temple on Mount Gerizim near Shechem, while the Judeans rebuilt their temple on Mount Zion in Jerusalem. Both believed their temple was the only correct place to worship God.

Relations between Jews and Samaritans were often difficult, which is what made this story so surprising—and helpful for John's situation!

The one where there's enough

THEY WERE SATISFIED

As told by Meredith J. C. Warren

This is a story about being hungry, and getting enough to eat. There are four ways of telling this story in the Bible, and here is another:

Jesus and his friends, the disciples, were tired. They had been traveling around the countryside teaching and healing, and they needed a rest. In those days people often walked to get around, and Jesus and the disciples had been walking for a long time. They got in a boat and sailed all the way across the lake, to try and find somewhere quiet.

But Jesus was very popular because he could make sick people better, and because people liked listening to him talk about God's message. He was so popular, goes the story, that even though he had tried to find somewhere out of the way, where people weren't likely to be, a big crowd—more than 5,000 people!—found him and gathered around, hoping that he would keep teaching them and healing them.

Instead of being angry at seeing them, Jesus felt sorry for them. After all, just like him, they'd walked a long way to get there, and they looked tired, too. Jesus healed the sick people in the crowd and spoke to everyone about God.

Then it started to get dark, and everyone started to get hungry. Hunger is a terrible feeling. Maybe you've been a little bit hungry, or maybe you are hungry a lot of the time? Maybe you know what it's like to not have enough food? Maybe you can imagine how the people crowded around Jesus and how the disciples felt when the sun went down, and they were far from their homes and kitchens.

The disciples started to get worried about their own hunger, and the hunger of the crowd. When you're hungry, worrying feels worse. They knew they didn't have enough food for all those thousands of people.

The disciples wanted Jesus to send everyone away. One of the disciples, Philip, knew it would be way too expensive to buy dinner for everyone. Even if they used all the money they had, it wouldn't be enough to buy even a tiny snack for all those people. They would all still be hungry, and the disciples would have no money left at all!

They thought Jesus should tell the people to go buy their own food with their own money and eat it by themselves. Jesus didn't like that idea—he had a miraculous plan in mind instead.

Just then, a child bravely came up to Jesus. They had brought some food along with them: five loaves of brown bread and two fish, just enough for them and their family to eat. But not nearly enough for that huge, hungry crowd. The child knew that sharing what you have is part of how God's love comes into the world, so they offered their bread and their fish to Jesus.

Jesus was very grateful for the child's kind offer. It can feel hard to share what you have, especially when you only have a little. Jesus took the bread from the child and blessed it.

Now here is the miracle part of the story: when Jesus broke the food into pieces and gave it out to that huge group of people, there was enough for everybody to eat! Just like when God fed the Israelites with heavenly bread called manna when they were escaping from Pharaoh in Egypt, the food Jesus gave to the crowd was enough for everyone to be satisfied.

In fact, there was more than enough. What started out as just enough food for the child and their family turned into enough food for over 5,000 people to eat, with leftovers! There were so many leftovers that they filled twelve baskets.

The story of this miracle is told in all four Gospels (with a few differences between them, of course). When Jesus fed the hungry thousands, it reminded people that, unlike their experience of being hungry and tired under Roman rule, God's kingdom provides enough for all people. The Gospel writers wanted people to understand that the full, happy feeling they have in their tummies when they have had enough to eat, is the same happy feeling God wants people to feel when they know God is looking after the world.

How Many?

After everyone had enough to eat, the disciples cleaned up the meal. They collected the leftover bread and fish in twelve baskets.

This number, twelve, isn't about counting the number of baskets in real life; instead, twelve is an important number that tells us something about the meaning of this miracle. It's a number that symbolizes completeness, because it reminds people of the twelve tribes of Israel, and the twelve lunar months in the year. That might be why Jesus often talked about having twelve disciples, even though everyone could see he really had a lot more than twelve disciples. The number twelve meant that all of God's people are included.

There are lots of these important symbolic numbers in the Bible. Seven is another important number that, like twelve, suggests wholeness. The first creation story in Genesis takes six days plus a seventh day of rest; when Jesus dictates the letters to the churches in Revelation, there are seven of them. And Jesus uses the number 77, a multiple of seven, to teach about forgiveness; Jesus uses that important number to tell people to be forever forgiving.

If you look out, you'll find other symbolic numbers like twelve and seven: see if you can find the numbers forty, or ten, or four, as you're reading more, and think about how they might mean more than just counting.

The one where Jesus walks on water

WHAT KIND OF MAN?

As told by Camille Szramiak Arneberg

One day after Jesus was done teaching a crowd of people, he was feeling a little exhausted. You know that feeling you get after playing with your friends for a whole long day? So much fun! But so tiring.

Jesus needed to rest and get back some energy. Kind of like how we plug a phone into a charger when it dies so we can turn it back on. Jesus did something like that by spending time plugged into God's love. So he went up on a mountainside by himself to talk with God.

While Jesus was alone with God, his disciples got into their boat and went on ahead of him to the other side of the lake.

Perhaps the wind this particular night started off quiet and calm. But later, as the little wooden boat made its way across the water, the wind began to blow fiercely.

Jesus's friends were surprised and they became frightened. Have you ever heard the wind howling at night? Wind can blow so strongly it will rattle your windows and be quite scary! Jesus's friends' hearts started racing and they felt knots in their stomach. They clung to each other and gripped the edges of the boat in fear.

The gusts of wind created big waves on the water, and the boat was tossed back and forth, back and forth. They held on for dear life.

The wind and waves raged on through the night, tossing the little wooden boat in the middle of the lake.

Then just before the sun started to rise, the disciples saw someone coming toward them…walking on the water! They were terrified!

What do you think they thought it was?

"It's a ghost!" they cried out in fear.

But it wasn't.

Jesus did not want them to be afraid so he called out to them right away. "Take courage," he said. "It's me, Jesus! Do not be afraid."

Peter, one of the disciples, called back to Jesus and said, "If it's really you, tell me to come out to you walking on the water."

So Jesus said, "Come."

And do you know what Peter did? He got out of the boat! But the boat was still in the middle of the water.

Peter didn't seem to care. He placed one foot on the now calm and shiny surface of the water. He didn't really know how, but he trusted that if Jesus called for him to come, then Jesus would make a way for him to get there.

One step on the water turned into two. Then two steps turned into three. Peter kept his eyes on Jesus and took one small baby step after another toward him. As he looked in Jesus's eyes, he knew that he could trust Jesus, even if he didn't know the "hows" and "whats" behind what was happening.

Suddenly, a strong gust of wind blew across the water again. It had been so calm. Where did that come from?!

Peter grew afraid. He stopped looking at Jesus and looked instead at the big waves. And at his friends in the little boat, violently tossing and turning again. His eyes grew wide. His hands got sweaty. His stomach turned. Fear crept through his entire body. When Peter took his eyes off Jesus, things got scary fast.

Peter panicked. And when he panicked, he started to sink. The enormous waves were surely more powerful than the kind eyes and presence of Jesus, Peter probably thought.

The water began to cover Peter's ankles… "Save me!" he called out to Jesus.

Jesus didn't wait a single second—he immediately reached out his hand to pull Peter up out of the water.

Jesus looked at Peter kindly and said, "Oh friend of small faith! Why did you begin to doubt my power?"

They climbed into the boat with their friends, and the wind and waves calmed down again. Even creation obeyed Jesus. The laws of nature just bent before him. The waters moved when and where he wanted them to. Regular ol' people can't walk on water (so don't try it!)—what kind of man was Jesus?!

Their friends in the boat were amazed. This is no ordinary man, they thought. "Surely, this must be God's son!" they said.

Mark

The Gospel of Mark is likely the oldest of the four Gospels. In fact, many people who study the Bible think Matthew and Luke read Mark's Gospel before they wrote their own.

Matthew and Luke tell lots of the same stories that we find in Mark's Gospel. (We don't need to mention that his name probably wasn't Mark, do we? You know how this works!) But Matthew and Luke often add things to Mark's stories—for example, Mark's Gospel doesn't mention Peter walking on water in this story, but Matthew's Gospel does.

Sometimes Matthew and Luke add the SAME extra bits to their Gospels. This made people wonder whether they both read another collection of stories or sayings of Jesus—one that is now lost, but would have been shared widely among Jesus followers. Or perhaps Luke read Matthew, and retold some of the stories found there with other stories he had heard. Either way, there are lots of similarities—and differences!—between Matthew, Luke, and Mark.

Mark's Gospel seems to have been written during a time of suffering, maybe in Rome when things got very bad for followers of Jesus for a while, or perhaps during the First Jewish Revolt, when the temple was destroyed. Either way, Mark wants his readers to know that good will come from their suffering, and God will make things right.

LUKE 10:25-37

The one with the good neighbor

HEY THERE, NEIGHBOR

As told by Shane Claiborne

———————

One day, a super smart expert in the law met Jesus. He wanted to see how smart Jesus was, but he also wanted Jesus to see how smart he was. "Teacher," the man said, "what must I do to get in on this eternal life thing?"

Jesus knew the expert knew the law back to front, so he replied, "What does the law say about how you get to experience life eternal?"

The expert gave a really good answer in response. He quoted two epic verses from the law, one from Deuteronomy and the other from Leviticus:

> "Love the Lord your God with all your heart and with all your soul and with all your strength and with all your mind; and, love your neighbor as yourself."

"Boom. Exactly. That's it." Jesus said. "Do this and you will experience life eternal." But the expert had more questions. "And who is my neighbor?" he asked. When someone asks "who is my neighbor" they could also ask "who is not my neighbor." That is, who do I—and don't I—have to love. Where are the boundaries?

So Jesus responded with a story…

> "A man was walking down the road from Jerusalem to Jericho. As he was traveling, some guys attacked him and stripped off all of his clothes. They were really mean, and they beat him up so bad he was unconscious. Then they left him bleeding and alone, lying in a ditch. Now, this was a well-traveled road, so eventually some

other people saw the man. One of them was a famous pastor of a big church. He had written lots of books and was often on TV. But he didn't even stop to check if the man was okay. Maybe he was late to his church service, or maybe he was scared the bullies were still around.

(Okay…this isn't exactly how Jesus told this story, because there were no TV preachers in Jesus's day. There were no TVs! Or books. But we can imagine how Jesus might update the characters in this story if he was talking to us today, so that's what we're going to do.)

Along came another guy. He was also a religious man. He was a Bible teacher at a college, who had written over 30 books about God and the Bible. Some of them were even best-sellers. He was texting on his phone and had his earbuds in. He saw the man, but he didn't stop to help either. Maybe he was late to a birthday party or had to teach a class.

Now there was one more fellow that came down the road. This guy wasn't really very religious at all—at least, the TV preacher and Bible teacher wouldn't have thought so. But as this man walked along the road, he noticed the man in the ditch and his heart broke. He had no idea who the man was—the man had no clothes on and could not speak, so the kindly man could not even guess who he was or where he was from. He wasn't even sure if the guy was still alive, that's how badly he had been injured.

But this man was deeply moved with compassion for the man in the ditch. He thought to himself, 'This could be me…or my son. Or my grandma. I've got to do something.' So he bandaged up the man's wounds using his own clothes and whatever else he could find. He even used the water in his water bottle to wash the man's wounds (and this was in the desert!). He was concerned that the man was naked, and thought, 'I sure wouldn't want someone to see my naked body!' So he took off his sweater and put it over him, even though he was a little chilly. Then he placed the man on his donkey, and took him to the nearest town, where he found a little bed and breakfast place. But he didn't stop there. He took out some money and gave it to the family who ran the B&B and said, 'Please take care of this brother, and if it costs you more than this, I'll pay you back when I come back through town in a few days.'"

Jesus looked at the expert who had asked him the question and said, "Which of these three men do you think was a neighbor to the man who was beaten by the bullies?"

And the expert said, "The one who had mercy on him."

Then Jesus said, "Go and do likewise."

The one about being present

WHAT IS BETTER?

As told by Marika Rose

Mary was just sweeping the last of the dust out of the house when she spotted Jesus walking toward the home she shared with her sister Martha. She was so excited to see him but she knew it wasn't her job to officially welcome him into their home, so she ran to get her sister Martha.

Martha went out to greet Jesus with a huge smile on her face. But behind the smile her mind was whirring. She and Mary had been working hard all day, and although it was exciting to see Jesus, she couldn't help but think of all the new tasks she'd have to add to her to-do list. They had planned to eat a very simple meal, but that wouldn't do for someone as important as Jesus. She would have to start cooking immediately, and make sure there was a comfortable place for everyone to sleep. She should probably send a message round to Jesus's other followers in the town and invite them to come and join the celebratory meal. Maybe she could ask some of the others to bring some food with them. But could she even squeeze everyone in?

Running a household was a lot of work, especially when you couldn't afford to pay people to help you.

Martha wasn't just responsible for running her own household, she was also very busy trying to nurture the small community of Jesus's followers in Bethany, organizing their meetings, and trying to pass on Jesus's teachings to her neighbors. She was tired. Her feet and her back hurt, and her head was beginning to ache. A small part of her wished that Jesus hadn't come at all.

Unlike her sister, when Mary saw Jesus she completely forgot about all of the things that needed to be done. "I have so many questions for you!" she said, settling down at his feet. "I've been talking to everyone round here about the story that you tell about the sower who sowed his seed on the rocky ground, but the more I tell it, the more questions I have."

Jesus smiled at Mary, as pleased to see her as she was to see him, and the two were soon deep in conversation.

Martha watched the pair of them, anxious about all of the things that she needed to do. As their conversation continued, Martha became more and more frustrated at how irresponsible her sister Mary was being. Soon she could not contain her annoyance any longer.

Martha walked up to Jesus and said, "Lord, do you not care that my sister has left me to do all the work by myself? Tell her then to help me. Someone has to prepare the food so that we can give you a meal suitable for such a great teacher. Someone has to make sure that there is space for everyone to sleep tonight. I can't do everything by myself!"

Jesus looked up from his conversation, and his face softened as he looked at Martha. "Martha, Martha," he said, "you are worried and distracted by so many things. But you don't need to do all this extra work to show me that you love and honor me—I already know that. Let's just make a simple meal together—I'll help—and we can make sure that we've done the few things that are absolutely necessary. But Mary is right: we should spend as much time as we can on what's really important—being together and learning about the good news I bring."

Martha's annoyance began to fade.

Jesus smiled and continued, "Tomorrow all of the work that you do will be undone and you'll have to start over again. The floor will need sweeping, the beds will need making, and the dinner will need cooking. There will still be meetings to organize, money to keep track of. You'll keep needing to dust off your sandals to go and pass on my teachings to other people. But the time we spend together will stay with you forever, and nothing will be able to take that away. Don't you know that I have come to give you rest?"

Well, that's weird...

People have always told stories that help us think about our own lives, and we often see ourselves in the stories' characters. When a story is very popular, it gets told over and over again. Often the people telling the story make small changes so that their audience can better understand how it might relate to their lives.

The story of Mary and Martha must have been very important to early followers of Jesus, because we have several copies of the same story with slightly different details.

In some of these versions, when Martha confronts Jesus, Jesus says that only a "few things" are necessary. In others, he says just "one thing" is necessary.

So how do we know what Jesus actually said? We don't! Just as there are four different Gospels telling the stories of Jesus's life in four different ways, there are also multiple versions of each Gospel story, gathered from the many different copies of the Gospels that were passed around by the early church communities.

So we make choices. I've chosen to use "few things" here, because I think it's important to remember that some of the things Martha is worrying about really are important. For example, I get very grumpy if I haven't had a proper meal! Do you?

The one about God's never-ending love

REJOICE WITH ME

As told by Savannah Locke

———

Jesus took a deep breath and looked at the crowd surrounding him. It was filled with so many different kinds of people. Some in the crowd were very good at being good! They loved doing the right thing and being faithful to God. Others were a little lost. They didn't know what it was like to walk with God yet. Jesus was so happy they were there.

When the good ones saw how Jesus befriended the lost, they were upset and asked, "Why is Jesus welcoming them, too?!"

Jesus heard their frustration and told three stories to demonstrate how much God loves finding lost things. The first story was about finding a lost sheep. The second was about finding a lost coin. And the third? Well, the third was about a man with two sons...

The man's older son was responsible and wise. He worked alongside his father day after day, from before the sun rose until long after the sun set. He never complained or asked for anything because he loved his father and was happy to help. But the younger son...

Well, one day, the younger son asked for his inheritance. An inheritance is a gift some parents leave for their families when they die. It could be money, land, or special things they owned. It was unusual to ask for an inheritance before someone died. This might have hurt the father's feelings, but surprisingly, he said yes and divided up his wealth.

The younger son took the money and ran away to a distant land, leaving everything he knew behind. With his newfound wealth and freedom, he went wild! He did what he wanted, when he wanted. Before he knew it, he had wasted his inheritance until every last penny was gone. To make matters worse, a famine struck the land where he was living.

He went from having lots of money to having none. He went from feeling full to feeling hungry. How would he survive? He needed a plan to make it through.

So the younger son found a job feeding pigs in a nearby field. He was so hungry, he dreamed of filling his stomach with pig food! He was lost and it was all his fault. Maybe this was the end of his story.

Then, out of nowhere, he had a wild thought: "Wait a minute! Even the workers at my father's house have food to spare, but here I am—his son!—starving to death! What if I return to my father and ask to be a servant? I might finally feel full again." No, he couldn't go back—could he?

He was out of options and decided to return home. He thought he had done too many bad things to be called "son" but at least he would have food and shelter as a servant.

He wrote a speech on the way back, hoping his father would listen: "Father, I turned against you and I don't deserve to be called your son, but please let me work for you."

Before he knew it, the terrain around him looked familiar. If he squinted, he could see the outline of his old house in the distance. He also noticed a strange shadow moving toward him. Maybe a farm animal got loose? Or maybe it was just his imagination?

As the shadow got closer and closer, he realized it was his father running towards him!

The second the father reached his son, he wrapped his son up in a big bear hug. The younger son quickly blurted out his speech: "Father, I turned against you and I don't deserve—"

But the father wouldn't have it! His son was home! He called out to his servants, "Quick! Dress my son in the best robe! Get him a ring and sandals! And let's throw a massive party to celebrate! Rejoice with me! For this son of mine was lost but is now found!"

The celebration began. Everything was right in the world, except…well… remember the older son?

The older son who worked hard for his father? Who did everything right? No one threw him a party. The older son could not understand why his father would welcome his lost brother…and forget about him. Feeling hurt and overlooked, he refused to join the party.

His father went and found him. "Son," he said, "you are always with me, and all that is mine is yours." The father looked at his son with compassion and love. He was proud of him and wanted him to experience the joy of his brother being found.

Jesus finished the story and looked at the crowd. Some people were sad, because they felt like the older brother who felt forgotten. Others had eyes filled with tears, because they felt like the younger brother who was lost and welcomed home. But Jesus knew God was a faithful father who would always run to all of them with never-ending love.

The one where fair isn't always just

IT AIN'T FAIR

As told by Miguel A. De La Torre

Jesús had a problem. You see, many people believe that time equals money. If you work one hour, you receive one hour of pay. If you work two hours, you receive two hours of pay. And if you work a whole day, you receive a full day's wage. Now that's fair, right?

But Jesús was more interested in justice than he was in fairness. How could he explain a way of living that is just for everyone? Looking at his followers, Jesús began to tell them a story…

Once upon a time there was this vineyard owner who needed workers to pick grapes. So, she woke up early in the morning, before the sun came up and the rooster crowed, to look for laborers. Many who worked on her farm were poor. Some were the children of immigrants, others were from another country and came so they could send money back home to their hungry families. This was hard work, under a hot sun. At the end of the day, their backs would hurt from being hunched over the vines cutting clusters of grapes.

The vineyard owner arrived at a day workers' center where she saw several people just standing about, talking and laughing among themselves.

"Hey amigos," the vineyard owner asked, "Do you want to go to my farm and pick grapes? If you do, I will give you a full day's pay!"

They all said "Sí"—which means "yes"—and went straight to work.

Later, around 9am, she saw some laborers standing outside the hardware store.

"Do you want to work at my farm?" the vineyard owner enquired.

"Sí" they responded, and off to work they went.

Around noon, when the vineyard owner was hungry and decided to have lunch at a taqueria that served delicious homemade tacos, she noticed some workers also eating lunch. The vineyard owner asked them if they were looking for work. They all said yes, so she hired them on the spot. After finishing their meals, they, too, went off to pick grapes.

At 3pm, when the vineyard owner went to buy grocery items, she noticed some workers just standing around near the bodega. They were sad because they had been looking for work all day long but were unable to find any. Without a job, they would not be able to feed their families that day. When the vineyard owner saw them, she told them not to worry, but to go to her farm and pick grapes. They left happy that they finally found some work!

At the end of the workday, the vineyard owner went to her farm to make sure everyone got paid. It is so important that everyone gets paid on time and is not forced to wait. The vineyard owner was so pleased because many grapes were picked that day. Everyone had worked very hard.

All her employees stood there—tired and sweaty—but glad to have found work. Their children would not go hungry tonight!

The vineyard owner paid those who started working at 3pm a full day's wage. She did the same for those who went to work at noon and at 9am. Then she paid those who showed up early in the morning, paying them the same amount—a full day's wage.

Do you think this is fair?

Some of the workers thought it was unfair. After all, they worked more hours than those who came to the vineyard just before the end of the workday. They should get more money, they grumbled among themselves. For them, the vineyard owner's actions were not fair because they believed that time equals money.

But the vineyard owner was more interested in justice than fairness. She explained that only a cruel and unjust employer would send their workers away with not enough money to meet their basic needs. Everyone who worked, no matter for how long, must leave with enough money so that they and their families could eat and have a place to sleep.

After telling this story, Jesús turned to the crowd and explained that the last will be first and the first will be last. It should not matter what time people show up because everyone can expect justice from the righteous employer; everyone can expect to leave with enough to survive another day.

The point is...

Rules, rules, rules. Rules are everywhere. Some rules are good because they keep us safe—"Don't talk to strangers," or "Don't touch a hot stove." But sometimes the rules can be used as an excuse not to do what is just, especially when we're speaking about things that are hard to understand, like what justice is, or what God is like, or how should we treat others.

If all we do is follow rules—this is called legalism—we might miss why the rules exist in the first place. So Jesús, who was a brilliant teacher, taught the reasons for rules through parables. A parable is a made-up story that helps people better understand a difficult truth about how to live life. They were designed to teach what justice is, who God is, and how we are to treat each other.

When Jesús told the story of the vineyard owner, he showed his listeners that the rule to pay workers their wages is about more than just time equals money— it's about ensuring everyone has enough money to live. The story shows us that the employer has a greater responsibility toward their workers.

God's kin-dom rules are not like those of the kingdom ruling the lands Jesús and his friends lived in. Unlike the empire of that time, Jesus talked about a society where everyone is treated justly. The moral of this story was true then, and it is still true today.

The one where Zacchaeus follows Jesus

MAKING THINGS RIGHT

As told by Raj Nadella

———

There once was a man named Zacchaeus who lived in Jericho and collected taxes for the Roman Empire. Zacchaeus got very rich by collecting a lot more taxes than the Roman Empire asked for and keeping the rest for himself. These heavy taxes made life miserable for many people, so it is not suprising that Zacchaeus was not a popular man. In fact, he was deeply unpopular.

Zacchaeus heard everyone in Jericho talking about this cool new messiah called Jesus. He really wanted to see this Jesus, but there was a big problem: he was short and could not see past the massive crowd that surrounded Jesus. Jesus wasn't all that tall either, so Zacchaeus could not catch a glimpse of him.

Guess what Zacchaeus did?

He got creative and came up with a plan to get around the problem. He asked around and found out where Jesus was heading. Then he ran ahead, and just like he did when he was a child, he climbed up a tall sycamore tree. He hid along a thick branch, hoping no one saw him. Zacchaeus wanted to see Jesus without being seen. And he waited.

Jesus slowly made his way to that tree and stopped for a moment. And Zacchaeus's heart stopped for a moment. He took a good look at Jesus from high on that branch. And then the most incredible thing happened. Jesus looked up and said, "Howdy, Zacchaeus, come on down. We need to talk."

Wait, what? Zacchaeus could not believe that Jesus knew his name. Then Jesus added, "I want to stay at your home tonight."

Holy moly! Jesus just invited himself to dinner at his home. Zacchaeus pinched himself hard to make sure he wasn't dreaming. Then he said "yes" three times really fast!

The crowd watching this could not understand what Jesus was doing. He has been serving the poor so faithfully throughout his ministry. Now he was going to eat and stay with someone who got super rich by basically stealing from the poor. Why would a respected person like Jesus want to stay with a corrupt tax collector? Was Jesus just pretending to care about the poor?

Not at all.

You see, Jesus knew that God's reign included all kinds of people, even really unpopular ones like Zacchaeus.

But what would Jesus and Zacchaeus talk about at dinner? Would Jesus encourage Zacchaeus to be kind to the poor?

We don't know! The people who wrote Luke do not tell us what Jesus and Zacchaeus talked about that night, but we do know what happened next.

Zacchaeus told everyone he was going to pay back the money he took from them. But not just the money he actually took—he would pay back four times as much money as he stole. And he would donate half of all his money to the poor.

The crowd was in utter disbelief. It was so quiet, you could have heard a pin drop.

"Is this really Zacchaeus talking this way?" they asked. The Zacchaeus they knew had exploited the poor at every turn. It was radical—almost unthinkable!—for him to give away half of his riches and return the money he took, not once but four times over. He was about to lose thousands of denarii—almost all of his money. The super wealthy Zacchaeus would be poor. And he seemed totally jazzed about it.

But that's what happened when Jesus transformed Zacchaeus's heart and values. Jesus knew that making things right is not just about saying sorry for our mistakes; it means we reverse our wrongs in every way. That's what Zacchaeus did. When his heart changed, so did the way he treated people. And this transformation in Zacchaeus made Jesus so happy.

"Today salvation has come to Zacchaeus's house," declared Jesus.

In Luke's Gospel, Jesus saves people throughout his life, just as he does for Zacchaeus. For Luke, salvation is not an idea or something super spiritual that happens to you; it is also something that happens in you. For the writers of Luke, salvation is about how we relate to God, but it is also about how we relate to each other. It is about how we treat others in our everyday interactions, big and small. Salvation is about making things right.

Luke

Would it surprise you to know that we don't know who wrote the Gospel According to Luke? No, of course not, because you know that the Gospel writers did not leave us their names. But the writers of Luke's Gospel did dedicate this Gospel to someone—Theophilus!

Unfortunately, we do not know who Theophilus was either. "Theophilus" means "God-lover" in Greek, so Theophilus might have been one person or a whole group of people.

What we do know is that there are a number of stories in Luke's Gospel that do not appear in any of the other Gospels. And these stories tell us quite a bit about what "Luke" wanted us to know about Jesus and who they were writing for.

Many of the stories Luke shares focus on poor, hungry, oppressed, excluded, and forgotten people—the people others often left out. Or on wealthy people who act justly. For Luke, part of the good news of Jesus—and the reign of God—was that everyone would have what they need and people would treat each other justly. How we use our money and resources mattered to Luke.

Many scholars believe the author(s) of Luke wrote for a community of Gentiles living outside of Judea. Perhaps people with power or money, who wanted to follow Jesus well. Stories about people like Zacchaeus showed them what that looked like.

MATTHEW 22:1-14; LUKE 14:15-24

The one about the kingdom of heaven

A VERY BIG PARTY

As told by Richard Rohr

One day, Jesus was teaching when the conversation turned to the kingdom of heaven. People had lots of ideas about the kingdom of heaven back then— what it was, who got to be part of it, and what you had to do to "get in." (A lot like today, really!) So Jesus told the people a story to show them what the kingdom of heaven is like, and it went like this...

Once upon a time, a certain man prepared a huge banquet and invited all of his friends.

When the table was set and the food was ready, the man sent his enslaved servants out to gather all of his friends who had been invited but...they didn't come! One said he had to tend to his farm. Another said he had to work. And another said he could not come because he just got married.

The man's enslaved servant came back and told the man what had happened.

The man's heart was broken. His body burned with shame and anger. His friends had rejected his invitation.

So he said to his enslaved servants, "Everything is ready, but my friends aren't coming. So go into the streets and invite everyone you see to the party. Invite the people who are poor and those who cannot walk. Bring back the blind and those who are maimed. Gather everyone you find and let's fill this house for a party!"

And they did. They invited everyone they saw: People who were poor and those who could not walk. People who were blind and those who were maimed. Young people and old people. Tidy people and messy people. Locals and out-of-towners. Rule-followers and rule-benders...everyone!

Then everyone who said yes made their way to the banquet where they ate, drank, danced, laughed, and celebrated. And so the hall—and the man's heart—were full of gladness.

****

God has always had a very hard time giving away God: No one seems to want this gift. We'd rather have religion, and laws, and commandments, and obligations, and duties. I'm sure many of us attend church out of duty, but gathering with other Jesus followers is supposed to be a feast.

Do you know how many times in the four Gospels eternal life is described as a banquet, a feast, a party, a wedding, the marriage feast of the Lamb? Fifteen!

Do you know how many parables there are about eternal life being a courtroom or a judgment scene? One. Matthew 25.

And that's good. We need Matthew 25 because it makes it very clear that the most important issue is how we care for those who are poor and marginalized.

But we forget this good news of Jesus, sending a message out to the highways and the byways, inviting everybody who's willing to come to the banquet. It's that simple!

Jesus goes out of his way to mention the good and the bad alike.

We might not like that either. We might only want the good people to be there at the banquet, assuming, of course, that we're the good people. Have you ever thought about how silly that is? Do you realize that every religion thinks that they are the ones that God likes?

And we end up gathering at the party thinking we're better than everyone else; but when we do, it resembles something that very often isn't much like a party. Let's be honest and admit that some days, we might not be excited to be at church. For many of us, the Body of Christ is not a party.

Instead, we might believe that heaven is a giant courtroom scene. The good people win, the bad people lose, and almost everybody is bad except our group.

That won't work! It gives no joy and no hope to the world. It tells people they're on the right side when sometimes they're very unloving people who don't care about those who are poor or marginalized at all. And sometimes Christians are no better than anybody else, in fact, very often—I'm sorry to say it—we're worse.

Do we want to be a part of the feast to which all are invited? The only people who don't get in on the party are those who don't want to come—so I guess we have to ask ourselves, "Do we want to come?"

MATTHEW 21:1-16; MARK 11:1-18; LUKE 19:28-48; JOHN 12:12-19

The one where Jesus enters Jerusalem

A FUNNY KIND OF KING

As told by Jarrod McKenna

Now was the time the Jewish people celebrated the holiday of Passover! Crowds poured into Jerusalem singing psalms, remembering when God defeated Pharaoh and freed the people from slavery in Egypt. And those people in the crowds all held one very special hope: that now was the time God would free them again!

But the Roman Emperor Caesar Tiberius was having none of it. Roman soldiers were all over Jerusalem to "keep the peace" and kill any dream of freedom. The presence of the world's most powerful army sent the people a clear message: "Sing your songs. Tell your stories. Chant your prayers. But don't think for a moment they can move the most powerful empire in the world. We have taken your land! We have taken your wealth! We even control your holy temple! You say your God of Deliverance dwells there? Here's what we know is in your temple: the records of who owes us how much, and the leaders we pay to do what we want. There is only one king, one son of God, one savior, and one Lord—Caeser Tiberius, the Roman emperor!"

From the west, Caesar's representative, Pilate, rode into Jerusalem with what must have looked like a sea of soldiers on powerful war horses. Like Pharaoh's army that chased Moses and Miriam and all of those enslaved in Egypt, here was unbeatable military might. Here was the glory of the world's most powerful king, shining swords and shields! A dust cloud of fearsome warriors marching to the drums of war! Reminding every worshipper in the temple of one thing: Caesar is Lord, the world's true king, and Rome brings peace through the sword.

So what did Jesus do? As he wept over the city in prayer, he had a plan Jesus told his disciples to go into a village and find a donkey. Then Jesus said, "If anyone asks, 'Why are you taking this little donkey?' Just tell them, 'The Lord needs it but we'll bring it back.'"

Can you see the surprise on their faces?! Can you hear them thinking, "Which Lord? Not Caesar! Wait! Does he mean God's true king? Is it like the prophet Zechariah's poem,

> Rejoice greatly, O Daughter of Zion!
> Shout, Daughter of Jerusalem!
> See your king comes to you,
> just and bringing liberation,
> nonviolent and riding on a donkey,
> on a colt, the foal of a donkey.

So the disciples brought the little donkey to Jesus and Jesus rode that little donkey from the east toward Jerusalem. Jesus was making fun of rulers and their war horses and their empires built on violence, showing the crowds that God's kin-dom is nothing like that. And everyone got Jesus's joke straight away.

People took off their cloaks and spread them on the ground with palm branches, laying them before the donkey. Then they sung out,

> Deliver us! Blessed is he who comes in the name of the Lord!
> Blessed is the coming kingdom of our ancestor David!
> Hosanna in the Highest!

Jesus is a funny kinda king.

But Jesus was only getting started. As he entered Jerusalem, Jesus went to the temple and cased the joint. Then he and the twelve disciples went back to Bethany to pray.

The next morning Jesus messed up the temple with a protest that disturbed everything but hurt no one. Tables were flipped! Doves went flying! The animals that were there to be killed went running for safety! Those doing the buying and selling ran off as well.

Then Jesus addressed the crowd using the poetry of the prophets,

My house will be called
a house of prayer for all people.
Yet you have made it a den
for those who steal then go there to hide!

It was at this point that those who thought Jesus was a threat decided
something must be done. They weren't laughing at this funny kind of king: a
king who disturbs the peace to tell the truth and saves on a donkey, never a war
horse. They weren't laughing at all.

The one with the servant king

DO THIS & REMEMBER

As told by Marlena Graves

———————

Before Jesus died, he and his disciples had one last dinner together. That night, Jesus did something his disciples considered rather strange at the time. Now they did not know it was Jesus's last dinner, but even so, they thought it was strange. And maybe you would consider it strange too! Jesus took off his outer robe, so as not to get it dirty, grabbed a towel and a bowl of water, bent down, and began washing his disciples' dirty, stinky feet!

Have you ever gotten a whiff of someone's smelly feet? Maybe they had socks on, and their feet began to sweat so much that their feet emitted the putrid vinegar-like smell of stinky soccer socks and shoes. Have you had a friend or sibling stick their stinky feet or socks in your face? Yuck! Maybe you went outside barefoot, to play or to do chores, just to return with your feet caked in mud, or worse. Maybe your parent or guardian snapped, "Don't walk in here with your muddy feet! Don't bring mud into the house!"

Well during Jesus's time on earth, people often wore sandals, if they had any shoes at all. Of course, they did not have the types of shoes and boots that we have today. They did not wear socks. Whenever they traveled down a dirty dusty road to visit friends, to go into town, or whenever they ran outside to play, their feet got dirty. Sometimes they got animal dung on their feet because animals also used the same roads. Animal dung, dust, and mud on your feet—yuck!

When Jesus began to wash Peter's feet, Peter cried out, "Jesus, don't do that! Stop it!" Now, why do you think Peter objected to Jesus washing his and the other disciples' feet? Because their feet were dirty? Well, yes. And because Peter thought Jesus was too important to wash his or anyone else's feet.

Jesus was God the Son and their teacher. In Jesus and through Jesus the earth, the whole universe, and everything that exists was created. You, me, plants, animals, the planets, and everything you find in outer space and beyond. Jesus was the savior of the world! The messiah. People should have been washing his feet! That's why Peter objected.

There are people who think they are more important than others and who want others to think of them as important. They show off. "Look at me! Look at me!" They want to be waited on, served, praised, and admired. But here we see that Jesus loved his disciples so deeply that he willingly did the dirty work, acting like the lowliest servant. He wasn't demanding that his disciples or other people make him the center of attention. Jesus didn't say "Look at me! Look at me! I have all the power! Aren't I so great?" He wasn't sitting on an earthly throne in a palace, in beautiful and expensive clothing, ordering people around with words like, "Servants! Do my bidding, or else!" Instead, Jesus showed love by doing the job none of his disciples wanted to do that night or ever—washing grubby, stinky feet.

Jesus washed each of the disciples' feet until they were all clean. Then he stood up, put his outer robe back on, and told them, "I have been an example to you. Now you go and wash other people's feet."

Is Jesus asking the twelve disciples and his disciples today to wash people's feet? Maybe, if the occasion calls for it.

However, what Jesus is saying is that we should never think or act like we are too important to lovingly serve others. Followers of Jesus ought to be known for lovingly serving others. It might look like listening to your parents or guardians, letting someone else go first in line, or not fighting with your siblings when you are sure you are right. If you are unsure about what it means to serve people like Jesus would, ask others who lovingly serve Jesus. They will be happy to offer ideas.

A Last Supper

The story of Jesus washing the disciples' feet only appears in the Gospel According to John. The Gospels According to Matthew, Mark, and Luke tell a very different story about Jesus's last meal with his disciples.

In Matthew, Mark, and Luke, Jesus shows his disciples a very special way to remember him. The details are a bit different in each of these stories (of course!), but in all three of them Jesus breaks some bread and says, "This is my body." He tells them to eat it and remember him.

Then he does the same with the wine. "This is my blood of the covenant," he says. Then he tells them to drink it and remember him.

Which actually, when you think about it, is a bit gross. But this is how Jesus asked his disciples to remember him and it's something churches of all traditions all around the world still do even now.

Today we call it "communion," "the Lord's Supper," or "Eucharist" (Thanksgiving)and it's a very special time for followers of Jesus. When people take communion, they are "one" with Jesus. They remember him. They remember that they are part of a big family that loves Jesus. And they remember all that Jesus taught and all that he did.

The one where Jesus prays

GETHSEMANE

As told by Bradley Jersak

After their last dinner together, Jesus and his friends went for a walk to one of their favorite spots. They left the city and crossed a valley to a place called the Mount of Olives. There is a beautiful olive garden on the side of that hill called Gethsemane.

Jesus told his friends to sit down and wait while he went to pray to his Father in heaven. He took three of his friends along with him: Peter, James, and John. There in the garden, he began to feel sorrow—a very heavy sadness—like holding all the sadness of everyone in the whole world all at once! He told his friends, "I feel so sad. It is like being lost and all alone in the dark. Please stay awake with me and pray. And pay close attention. Something is going to happen, so be careful to do only what God wants." I wonder if he was talking to Peter? I wonder what Peter will do or say?

Jesus walked a little farther away on his own. How far? Not too far. About as far as you can throw a stone. Jesus knelt down to pray on his hands and knees, all the way to the ground, with his face touching the grass. He began to pray, calling out, "Abba!" That's what Jesus called God. "Abba, this feels so hard, like drinking a giant cup of sorrow.
I know you can do anything. Is there any other way to save my friends? To heal the whole world? But if I have to drink it, I will. I will do whatever you want. I only want what you want."

Jesus knew his time on earth teaching his friends was coming to an end. His heart was full of sadness and grief, and maybe even a little bit of fear. Luke tells us God answered Jesus by sending an angel from heaven. God's angel didn't help Jesus escape. Instead, he helped him feel strong enough to drink the full cup of all that sorrow. After praying, Jesus got up and went back to his friends. He hoped they were praying and watching, but nope.

Zzzzzzzzzzz...

What?!

That's right! They were sleeping, right there on the grass. Jesus woke up Peter and said, "Peter, couldn't you stay awake with me? Not even for one hour? Please, please! Stay awake and pray so you don't get tempted." How would Peter and his friends be tempted? We'll soon see.

Jesus was still feeling very upset, so he went off alone to pray again. This time he prayed with even stronger feelings. "Papa! I wish I didn't have to drink this cup of sorrow. But now I know. If I have to drink it, I will. I will do whatever you want. I only want what you want." Jesus prayed like this three times. And every time he came back, he found his friends sleeping again. They were sad now, too. So sad that it tired them out and they couldn't keep their eyes open. They kept falling asleep and didn't know what to say to Jesus.

After the third time, Jesus saw that his friends were still sleeping. "Wake up!" he said. "The time has come! Something important is going to happen. I am going to be given to people who will do bad things to me. Get up!" He knew that his friend Judas was coming. Judas, who he taught so tenderly and carefully. Who he traveled with and shared food with. Judas was bringing people to arrest him. Judas knew Jesus often brought his friends here. That's how they found him.

Jesus turned from his friends and there stood Judas. Around Judas were chief priests, elders and servants, all of them watching. All of them waiting. Jesus's friends were wide awake now.

Then, something unexpected happened. Judas walked over and kissed Jesus. And the sorrow filled Jesus all over again. Because Judas's kiss did not say, "Hello, my friend! I love you." It said, "This is Jesus. Arrest him." The men around Judas moved quickly, but Peter was faster. He grabbed a sword and cut off a man's ear. (John tells us the man's name was Malchus. Luke tells us that Jesus healed him.) But Jesus did not want swords and clubs and fighting. Not amongst his friends, and not against his enemies. Not even when it could save his own life. "Put your swords away," he said.

Jesus knew that what was about to happen, had to happen. Talking to God made him feel strong. He would drink the cup of sorrow.

The one where Jesus dies

MY GOD, MY GOD

As told by Drew G. I. Hart

———————

After Judas betrayed Jesus, Jesus was brought before a temple leader named Caiaphas and a team of powerful men. These leaders planned to falsely accuse Jesus. They wanted to put an end to him.

One by one, people told lies about Jesus. When that didn't work, they said Jesus taught people to disobey the Roman Empire. Some accused Jesus of saying he was God. And some said Jesus claimed he was God's chosen one, sent to set things right. Everything they said was said to get Jesus in trouble with the Romans or with his people.

When the trial was over, police soldiers began to beat and mock Jesus. Many people today call this police brutality and the soldiers who beat Jesus were brutal. They even blindfolded him and made fun of Jesus as they hit him. Jesus felt sad, hurt, and all alone.

Peter watched as Jesus was treated unfairly. But he kept his distance, afraid of what would happen to him if people knew he was Jesus's friend. Eventually, he was recognized, but three times he told people that he didn't know Jesus! Peter did not act courageously. Right after the third time, a rooster crowed and Peter realized what he had done. He felt sad and cried.

The next morning, the leaders took Jesus to Pilate, a very powerful and cruel Roman leader. Since the Romans controlled Jesus's homeland with an army, Pilate could control whether Jesus lived or died. After asking some questions, Pilate couldn't find any reason to punish Jesus. So Pilate decided to let the crowd decide what would happen to Jesus. He told the people they could choose one person to set free from prison: they could pick Jesus or another prisoner named Jesus Barabbas.

Barabbas, like Jesus, wanted poor and hurting Jews to get free from under Rome. Barabbas was willing to kill and hurt others to get free, but Jesus taught his friends to love their enemies while they worked for freedom.

Jesus (Yeshua) means "savior." Who would the people trust as savior with their problems? Barabbas means "son of Father." Who was really God's chosen one—Jesus or Barabbas? The crowd had a big choice to make. Who would they set free? The crowd chose Barabbas. After all, Jesus was arrested without putting up a fight. Perhaps they wondered how loving their enemies could help get them free. The Romans and the powerful men seemed to have defeated Jesus. Pilate asked the crowd what he should do with Jesus. The crowd, influenced by powerful men, yelled, "Crucify him!" The Romans crucified people—hung them on a cross (wood posts in the shape of a "T" or a "t")—to end their life. They did this outside, where everyone could see, to scare people into obeying them.

Again, soldiers beat and bullied Jesus. They put a purple robe and a crown of thorns on Jesus. They made fun of him, calling him the "King of the Jews." They did not believe he was God's chosen one.

Then Jesus had to carry his own cross outside the walls of Jerusalem to a place called the Skull. The cross was large and very heavy. It was too heavy for Jesus to carry all the way, so the soldiers forced an African man named Simon to carry the cross the rest of the way.

At the place called the Skull, as people watched, Jesus and two others were each hung on a cross with nails. The cross hurt Jesus, and he felt alone and abandoned. Yet, Jesus had not given up on loving his enemies. He would not hate the people who did this to him. Instead, Jesus pleaded to God to forgive everyone who hurt him or wanted to end his life.

This is not how things were supposed to end for God's chosen one. People expected that God's chosen one would bring an end to Roman control and all the terrible things people do to one another. He would set things right. Instead, powerful people were still in control and they were doing terrible things to Jesus. That afternoon, Jesus cried out loud a song that was special to him and his people. He needed to express his feelings. His sadness. His feeling all alone. His hurt. As people watched, he cried out, "My God, my God, why have you left me?"

And with one last breath, Jesus's life was over.

The one where death is defeated

DO NOT BE AFRAID

As told by Elizabeth Schrader Polczer

After Jesus died, his friends were devastated. Most of them stayed home crying, and some of them were terrified that the same thing could happen to them.

But not all of his friends stayed home. One friend of Jesus loved him so much that she needed to be close to him again, even after he had died. This friend was Mary Magdalene. Mary and several other women stayed near Jesus when he was on the cross and were with him when he breathed his very last breath. They witnessed the whole awful sight.

After Jesus died, Mary and her friends saw that his body had been moved into a tomb in a nearby garden. Even though she wanted to stay by his body, she and her friends needed to go home because it was the Sabbath day. No work could be done on the Sabbath, because it was the day of rest.

But as soon as the Sabbath was over, Mary Magdalene ran straight back to the tomb of Jesus. Maybe she wanted to care for his body by anointing it with the customary herbs and spices, or perhaps she just wanted to sit down and cry near him.

When she arrived at the tomb, she received a big surprise: the tomb was open, and it was empty! Mary was scared. Thinking that Jesus's body had been stolen, she ran back to the other disciples and said, "Someone has taken Jesus out of the tomb! We don't know where they've put him!" A few of the men were also very upset, so they ran back to look at the tomb as well. Peter didn't know what to think of it, and he went home wondering what had happened.

When Mary returned to the empty tomb, she just cried and cried. All she wanted to do was to be near Jesus again, but now not even his body was here.

With tears streaming down her face, she looked inside the tomb, and she saw something peculiar. Now there were two angels sitting where Jesus's body had been—how strange!

They asked her, "Woman, why are you crying?" Confused and not knowing what to say, Mary replied, "They have taken Jesus away, and I don't know where they have put him."

Then she turned around because she could sense that a man was walking in the garden. Mary thought, 'Maybe he is the gardener and knows where Jesus's body has been taken.'

The man said, "Woman, why are you crying? Who are you looking for?" She replied, "Sir, if you have taken Jesus away, please tell me where you have laid him."

The man said to her, "Mary."

And right away she knew: it was Jesus! She exclaimed "Rabbouni!", which means "My Teacher!" Mary ran as fast as she could because she wanted to throw her arms around him. She wanted things to be just as they had been before.

But Jesus had an important job for Mary. He said to her, "Do not hold on to me, Mary. Instead, go to my brothers and tell them that I am returning to God, our Father."

Mary knew exactly what he meant; Jesus's "brothers" were all of their friends! Filled with love for Jesus, she did exactly as he asked. She ran through the dirt, the streets, and the alleys, back to their friends who needed to hear the news. Mary's heart was bursting! For a few moments on that first Easter morning, Mary Magdalene was the only person in the whole world who knew the good news. She was the whole church. She ran back to her friends and exclaimed: "I have seen the Lord!"

****

This is the story as it is told in the Gospel According to John. But there are other versions of this story too: Luke's Gospel says that Mary Magdalene had other women friends with her when she arrived at the tomb. Matthew's Gospel says that an angel told them not to be afraid: "Jesus is risen!" And both Mark and Luke say that it was the angel (not Jesus) who told Mary to go and share the good news with the others.

As Jesus stories were passed from person to person, the details of what happened on this extraordinary day were remembered and recorded differently. Soon many were sharing the stories of a great teacher and prophet—God's chosen one, the messiah—who defeated death...

A Towering Example

What does the name "Magdalene" mean?

There have been debates about Mary's nickname throughout history, and nobody is quite sure what it means. Some think she came from a town called "Magdala," which simply means "tower" (the Greek ending "-ene" refers to a female person). But there were many towns called Tower in ancient Palestine, and they always had another word included, such as "Tower of the Fishes" and "Tower of the Flock."

Some other people think that "Magdalene" was a nickname given to Mary. Saint Jerome wrote: "Mary 'the Magdalene,' who received the name 'toweress' because of her diligence and ardent faith, deserved to see the risen Christ first before the apostles."

Certainly Jesus gave nicknames to his closest disciples—Thomas was called "the Twin," and Peter was called "the Rock." So perhaps Mary Magdalene wasn't from a place called "Tower" after all—maybe Mary herself was a kind of tower of faith, which is was why Jesus appeared to her first on Easter morning.

The one with the Holy Spirit

A MIGHTY WIND

As told by Jennifer Garcia Bashaw

––––––––––

Dear Theophilus,

I wrote to you in my last letter about Jesus's life, about how he showed people what the kin-dom of God was like and invited them into God's new family. Now, I want to tell you how that new family got started and how the upside-down priorities of God spread to the ends of the earth.

You remember that on the third day after Jesus died, Mary Magdalene found the empty tomb and saw the risen Jesus for herself. According to the other disciples, the resurrected Jesus appeared to them as well.

Jesus taught many things during the weeks he was with the disciples. He reminded them of stories the people of Israel had told for centuries—stories that could help them understand the importance of his life, death, and resurrection. He also showed them that his resurrected body was real. Jesus was not a ghost, he was human—and more than that, he was the best human to ever walk the earth.

Before Jesus left his disciples to go to spend time with God, he gave them a challenge and a promise. He challenged them to be witnesses for the new kin-dom and to tell all the nations of the world about forgiveness and about the loving way of God. Then, he promised them a special kind of power from God that would come to them soon.

When that special power did come, it was quite the scene. It happened during the celebration of Shavuot (Pentecost), when many of the disciples were gathered together in a house—people like Mary, Jesus's mother, and other women disciples, along with John and James and Peter.

Now you may not know this, but normally at Shavuot the Jewish people thanked God for the land and the food they grew. They also remembered the time long ago when God made the covenant with Moses—when there had been thunder and lightning and fire on the mountain when God's presence appeared.

This Shavuot, while the disciples were celebrating how God showed up on a stormy mountain long ago, God showed up again. This time God did not appear on a mountain far away but right in the middle of them.

First, a booming sound like thunder filled the whole house where they were. But it wasn't thunder, it was the sound of a mighty wind whooshing into the room. After the wind, there was fire (or at least something that reminded them of fire) that seemed to hover over the heads of the disciples.

All of this, the booming and the whooshing and the flames, represented the different ways that God's spirit had showed up in the past. God's presence had come to God's people in many ways throughout the centuries: as a breath of life, as a burning bush, as a pillar of cloud and fire, and as a storm on a mountain. Now, the disciples were experiencing God's presence in all these ways all at once!

But that's not all that happened when God's spirit showed up. The disciples also started speaking in many languages. So many languages that they were able to be understood by all of the people who had come to Jerusalem for the holiday. So, Peter stood up in front of the crowds with a special message for the people.

"The Holy Spirit, the presence of God, has come to us today. You remember what the prophet Joel said: One day, God would pour the spirit onto all God's people. This spirit would give women and men, boys and girls—everyone!—the power of God. Jesus also promised that God's power would come to be with us. After God raised Jesus from the dead, Jesus went to be with God. But Jesus did not leave us alone. Everything that has happened today shows us that God is with us. Don't you see? Jesus is the Messiah."

The people who heard Peter's message wanted to become followers of Jesus. So, thousands of them decided to be baptized and they received the Holy Spirit just like the disciples had. That Shavuot day was the beginning of a movement that would spread quickly and expand the family of God all over the world. Christians today remember this amazing day as Pentecost.

The Holy Spirit

Just like the wind is invisible, the Holy Spirit is not something we can see. But, we can feel the wind and see its effects—the breeze on our face or the leaves swaying on the trees. We can feel the Spirit and its effects, too.

Some say the Spirit feels like peace or love inside them or that it helps them understand the world better. Some say the Spirit gives them courage to speak up for people or to do hard things. Some describe the Spirit as a power that fills them up and makes them shout or sing or speak words they don't know. (Some call this "speaking in tongues," which means speaking in other languages.)

The word "spirit" in the Greek language (the language Acts was written in) is *pnuema* —you can say it "puh-nooma" or just "nooma". The word that is used to describe the mighty wind that blew on Pentecost is *pnoē*. Those two words sound similar because the spirit is often described as a wind.

In the Hebrew Bible, the word "*ruach*" means breath, wind, or—you guessed it!—spirit. God's *ruach* hovered over the waters in the Genesis 1 creation poem, gives breath to all living things (Numbers 27:16), and rests on prophets and leaders, like Isaiah and David.

God's spirit was not new. But what was new in this story was that God's spirit was on so many people all at once: a sign that something new was beginning.

ACTS 8:26-40

The one where there's nothing to stop you

EVERYONE'S INVITED

As told by Rachel Mann

Following Jesus should be the easiest thing in the world. All you have to do is start followinWg him. To be part of his community, just take a deep breath, say yes to Jesus, and get baptized.

Maybe that's how it was for Philip, one of seven special people chosen to look after the poorer members of the church in Jerusalem. Philip, who in a sign of how close he was to Jesus, received a message from an angel: travel down to Gaza on the road from Jerusalem.

Philip was excited as he stepped out. He was following Jesus's call, after all. Though maybe he felt a little less happy the further he traveled on the road...

As he walked alone, perhaps he thought of Jesus's parable—the one about the man who was beaten by thieves and abandoned for dead as he traveled down another road towards another town. Roads weren't always safe places in Philip's day. Maybe this following Jesus thing was riskier than he'd thought...

As Philip traveled down the dusty road to Gaza, he saw a chariot. Maybe Philip thanked God that—at last!—someone had come along who could offer him a lift before he was attacked by thieves or wild animals.

Philip ran to the chariot, excited and hopeful—happy to be picked up by a person so important and powerful that they traveled in the ancient equivalent of a big fancy car.

Maybe it was then Philip did a double-take.

For the person he met was very grand indeed: a person in charge of all the money for the queen of Ethiopia. A person of power and position, who had been up in Jerusalem to worship God and was now heading home.

But, that wasn't the only reason for the double take…

For the person Philip sat down next to was not exactly the usual sort of person welcomed into religious community, or many other places in the Roman world. They were—for those who set the rules—an outsider.

Perhaps Philip looked at this person and considered getting out of the chariot. The angel might have told him to travel towards Gaza, but the message included nothing about hanging out with anyone like this.

Philip met a person who was a "eunuch" (pronounced "yoo-nuck"). It's not a word we use much now, though once upon a time it was quite common. A eunuch would have been viewed with suspicion by lots of people, for they did not fit into the right 'box' of either man or woman, boy or girl. They were seen as someone in between.

Wonderfully, though, the eunuch and Philip found a connection.

The eunuch had been on pilgrimage to Jerusalem and was hungry for knowledge: 'Who is the Lamb whose life was taken away from him?' And Philip, the good and faithful servant of Jesus, told his new friend the answer.

For whatever else Philip might have thought when he met the eunuch, Philip broke open the scriptures and shared the good news about Jesus. He told the eunuch how Jesus was the Lamb who came to share God's love and grace with everyone, and how anyone who wanted to be part of Jesus's new community could enter it through baptism.

As they traveled down the road together, they came to some water and the eunuch said, "Look, here is water! What is to stop me from being baptized?"

And Philip, the honored insider, looked at this person who—for all their worldly power—had no honored place in the life of faith. And Philip said, "Nothing. Nothing at all."

For Philip realized that the good news he had just shared came down to this: No matter who you are, no matter how much you've been treated as an outsider or told you are unworthy of love and grace, no matter—Jesus adores you and wants to be close to you.

So they went down into the water and Philip baptized the eunuch.

As soon as the wonderful deed was done, God sent Philip on his way.

But the eunuch was not sad when they did not see their new friend anymore, because they knew they were an outsider no more. They, who had never been seen as right or good enough, knew that there were no limits on God's love and they went on their way home rejoicing.

Who Is In...Continued

The conversation about who was one of God's people and who was not did not end when Jesus was born. And it did not end when the church was born, either. It just changed a bit.

Although the early followers of Jesus did not call themselves "Christians" (that name came later), they were still trying to figure out what it meant to be a follower of Jesus and who got to be one.

Many early followers of Jesus were Jewish—which makes sense, because Jesus was Jewish and so were most of the people he taught. But some were not and these people were called Gentiles. As more Gentiles began to believe in Jesus,

new questions were asked: Who got to be part of God's family? If you followed Jesus, did you also have to follow Jewish torah? Was faith in Jesus enough to be part of Jesus's family? Who was in and who was out?

The scroll of Isaiah that Philip and the eunuch studied spoke of a day when God would honor eunuchs with "a memorial and a name" and would bring foreigners to God's holy mountain with great joy. This story declares that day has arrived. Through Jesus, God extends an invitation to everyone and anyone, far and wide, inviting them into an eternal love and a kin-dom family.

REVELATION

The one where God is still at work

A REVELATION

As told by Terry J. Stokes

Many years passed, and those who knew and walked with Jesus began to grow old. Many had died—some of old age, but some well before their time in not-so-comfortable ways. Jerusalem's beautiful temple had once again been destroyed, this time by Roman armies, and those who loved and followed Jesus began to wonder when he would return for them. They thought that he would go to heaven and be right back, but here they were, many years later. Still living under Rome. Still suffering. Still waiting. Wondering where God was among all this pain.

One of these followers was John. John lived on an island far from his friends. Perhaps he was sent there by the Roman emperor as a punishment for something he had done. Or maybe he went there to share the good news of Jesus. We do not know why he was there, but we do know what happened to him while he was there.

God gave John a dream. A vision, actually. A revelation: a message from God. John saw a bunch of sights that were almost too incredible to put into words: creatures stranger than the ones from any fairy tale, glimpses of heaven. Even scary moments where God gets mad at injustice.

As soon as John woke up, he hurried to write down everything he saw. As he wrote, he realized that his vision told a story. And he realized that the story was actually two stories in one.

The first was the story of right now. (Well, not right now. It was the story of two thousand years ago—it was John's right now, not our right now.) It was the story of earth as John knew it—a place where powerful people acted out of greed and selfishness, and ordinary people suffered because of it.

The things in John's vision represented ideas and people and moments from the kingdom John lived in—his right now.

In his vision John saw four horses and their riders. There was a white horse and a black horse, but there was also a red horse and a pale green horse! The rider on the white horse carried a bow, like the Babylonian and Assyrian soldiers did when they tore through ancient Israel and Judah. The rider on the red horse carried a sword, like the Romans.

The point of the four riders wasn't that they were actually four people riding on horses. They were how John described poverty, war, suffering, and death. They came to earth to cause pain and disaster. They reminded John (and us!) that when people have power, but they do not have kindness, they create an unjust world where most people don't have what they need.

Next, John saw the earth tremble. The sun turned black, the moon turned red, and the stars of the sky fell to the earth. (This is how John gets our attention. And it does get our attention, doesn't it? It's kind of like saying "the wind howled all through the night." The wind doesn't actually howl! Wolves do. We might say the wind "howled" to describe how scary the wind is.)

But then one more rider showed up. He rode a white horse and his name was Faithful and True. It was Jesus!

He first showed up in John's vision as a gentle Lamb, but now he arrives as a king, riding in to put an end to everything bad. To create a new, more beautiful way for us to live.

John finished writing down his vision and decided to send it to seven churches full of people he knew and loved. He knew each church's strengths and weaknesses, their hopes and fears. He wanted them to think about what his dream meant for their right now and for the future.

He wanted them to know that God had not forgotten them. God was still working behind the scenes to bring justice to the world. That was the second story John's vision told.

John wanted those churches to remember that God would give them strength to keep going, even in the hard times. That God would reward them for staying true. That there was a new world coming, an eternal delight that would swallow up the pain they were experiencing.

Sadly, many of the bad things in John's world that were represented by beasts and horsemen in his dream are still big problems today. Things like poverty, war, suffering and oppression. But thankfully, many of the good things from his vision are real today, too.

John's vision reminds us that God will keep working to make these good things bigger and bigger until they are all there is. It will be a new beginning that will never end.

Hold Steady

The book of Revelation is weird. It's full of dragons and beasts and horses and scrolls and lamps and all sorts of things that make no sense and can be more than a little bit scary. For us, anyway.

But for the readers of John's letter, it was the things that the dragons and beasts and other scary creatures represented that haunted their dreams and darkened their days.

The book of Revelation is an apocalyptic text. This means it reveals something that is hidden. John's vision revealed God was at work behind the scenes.

Even though Rome was still in charge.

Even though the people still suffered. Even though they couldn't see it.

God was at work.

The empires of this world would be overthrown. There would be justice. There would be peace—not Rome's idea of peace, its Pax Romana—but real peace, God's peace.

The weird dragons and beasts allowed John to share his message of hope without Roman soldiers realizing what he was talking about. (Them!)

But his readers knew. They knew who the beasts were. And they knew what they had to do. Hold steady. Have faith. And wait...because God is at work.

The one where everything is made new

A NEW HEAVEN & A NEW EARTH

As told by Randy Woodley

———————

Have you ever stopped to think what would happen if time just stopped? Would it be the end of all things that we know? What would happen to all the people and other creatures that we have loved in this life?

God assures us that time never ends. We call that eternity.

But eternity isn't time like we know it right now. It's time lived in perfect togetherness with God and in perfect relationship with each other and all of creation. Without any sorrow or evil.

John saw a vision of a world made new, where all the great things that already exist in heaven joined together with this wonderful earth. And the old earth that we know now, became a new earth.

In his vision, John heard a voice say, "Look! I am making all things new!" And this is the newness that God showed him…

A new earth big enough to hold everyone and everything that ever lived.

Big enough for every creature in the whole community of creation.

Big enough for every person, animal, and bird who ever lived.

Every tree. Every insect. And every flower.

And, everyone in the new earth was happy there, forever!

****

What was even more special about the new earth John saw was that God walked among everyone. God's home was among his people and there was complete union between people and God.

In the new earth God wiped every tear from peoples's eyes and there was no more death or sorrow or crying or pain. All of these things were gone forever!

No one was at war. No one ever went hungry. And the earth produced everything that all of God's community of creation needed.

In his vision, John saw a city too, but it was no ordinary city. It was a beautiful city full of gardens and trees and plants that produced enough food for everyone to eat.

And in this city, there was no place of worship, like a church or a temple or a mosque, because God and Jesus already walked among everyone!

In this city, there was no sun or moon because God's beauty and Jesus—the light of the world—lit everything up instead!

Every person, including every people group, nation, or tribe who ever lived, lived peacefully alongside each other in the new earth.

They each brought their special giftings and everyone learned from one another and could find their way because the light God gave was enough for them all to see.

People who were very important and people who didn't seem important, all walked and lived together as equals in this great city.

And in the new earth, the gates of the city were always open for anyone to come in…and no one was ever turned away!

****

Although this sounds like a wonderful place in the future, John's vision helps us imagine how we can shape the earth we live in now to be more like the one in his vision.

You live and breathe to bring God's vision for peace, healing, love, joy, friendship, and beauty to the world and to those around you right now!

That's the kin-dom of God.
And you are invited to be part of it…

NOW WHAT?

We have reached the end of this book, but this is not the end of your journey with the Bible—it is just the beginning. The Bible is filled with many weird and wonderful stories, far more than we could include here. There are so many characters you haven't met yet, and so many storytellers whose voices you have not heard.

But reading these stories is just the first step.

Just like the Bible's storytellers, you are invited to read these ancient stories for your own time and place. What are the empires in your world? Who are the prophets? Do you know a Hagar? A Daniel? A Mary? A Zacchaeus? Where can you see God at work?

These are the conversations you are invited into. Conversations with the Bible's storytellers and all who came after them. Conversations with those you read the Bible alongside. And conversations with God.

This is why the Bible is sometimes called the "living word of God." Because every reader keeps these ancient conversations alive, re-reading these stories for their times and places. So, what are you waiting for?

Join in the conversations.

GLOSSARY

Assyrian Empire A mighty empire that conquered the northern kingdom of Israel in 721 BCE (or 722 BCE, we cannot be sure of the exact year). Israel the kingdom was destroyed, and those who survived the Assyrian armies fled to other lands, including Judah.

Babylonian Empire Another mighty empire, this one conquered the southern kingdom of Judah in 597 (or 598) BCE. The Babylonians took many Judeans into captivity (or exile) in Babylon, first in 597/8 BCE, and then again in 586 (or 587) BCE, when they laid siege to Jerusalem and destroyed the temple. These experiences of exile shaped both the people and many biblical texts.

Canaan The name of the lands later called the northern kingdom of Israel and the southern kingdom of Judah.

canon A set of texts (or books) that religious authorities agree are the set of texts that are sacred and authoritative for their faith. The texts within the biblical canon differ across different faiths and denominations.

Christian Not a word we see much in the Bible! A Christian is someone who believes Jesus is the messiah, and whose life reflects the life and teachings of Jesus.

Galilee A region that covers the northern lands in what was once the northern kingdom of Israel. Jesus was a Galilean and much of his ministry occurred in Galilee.

Gentile A person who is not Jewish.

Greek Empire A mighty empire that defeated the Persian Empire in the 4th century BCE. Greek language and culture were spread throughout this empire, and it is during this time that Hebrew texts were translated into Greek.

Hebrew The language most of the Torah, Prophets, and Writings were written in. Also, one of the names given to the ancient ancestors of the Jewish people.

Israel The name of one of the patriarchs in the Bible (also known as Jacob), the name of all of the people in the 12 tribes of Israel, and the name of the northern kingdom of Israel. Confusing!

Jew/Jewish From a translation of the word Yehudi, which means "from Judah." Many people who study religion think a Jewish identity developed in the period after the Babylonian exile, when what bound people together was their shared faith in God, their scriptures, and their religious practices, rather than a king or the kingdom they lived in.

Judah The name of one of the sons of Jacob, one of the 12 tribes of Israel, and the southern kingdom of Judah. Confusing!

Judea The Greek and Roman name for Judah.

messiah A translation of the Hebrew word "mashiach," which means "anointed." Under Roman rule, the people eagerly awaited a very special king—one sent by God and descended from King David—who would free the Jewish people from bondage and foreign rule. They called this person the "messiah."

Persian Empire The Persian Empire defeated the Babylonian Empire in the 5th century BCE and gained control of the lands previously known as the kingdom of Judah, which they renamed the province of Yehud. Under Persian rule, those exiled by the Babylonians were allowed to return home.

Roman Empire The Romans conquered most of the lands around the

Mediterranean Sea, including Judea, Samaria, and Galilee (in 63 BCE). There were several Jewish–Roman wars between 66 and 135 CE, during which the temple in Jerusalem was destroyed in 70 CE.

Samaria The capital city of the northern kingdom of Israel, and later, the name of the region that covered the southern lands of what used to be the northern kingdom of Israel.

scribe Someone who recorded and copied important political, religious, economic, and other significant events and texts in ancient times.

scroll A long piece of animal skin or papyrus that scribes wrote on and could roll up for easy storage and transportation.

temple In this book, "the temple" refers to the temple in Jerusalem. The temple was the center of religious life in Jerusalem and beyond. It was destroyed in the Babylonian siege of Jerusalem in 586/587 BCE, then rebuilt by the returning exiles (515/516 BCE). Under Herod the Great the temple was extended, however, it was destroyed by the Romans in 70 CE.

AUTHORS

René August *In the Beginning...*
Reverend René August is strategist, thought leader, disciple maker, speaker, author, trainer, and reconciler. She lives in Cape Town, South Africa, and works at Tearfund as a Global Peacebuilding Specialist.

Jared Byas *Eden*
Jared Byas is the author of *Love Matters More* and *Jonah for Normal People*. He oversees The Bible for Normal People organization and co-hosts both *The Bible for Normal People* and *Faith for Normal People* podcasts.

Mari Jørstad *In Our Image*
Mari Jørstad is an associate professor of the Hebrew Bible and Academic Dean at the Vancouver School of Theology. Her research focuses on ecology, land, migration, and belonging in the Hebrew Bible. She is the author of *The Hebrew Bible and Environmental Ethics: Humans, Nonhumans, and the Living Landscape.*

Jonathan Lewis-Jong *Re-Creation*
Originally from Malaysian Borneo, Fr. Jonathan Lewis-Jong now finds himself as an Anglican priest in West Sussex in the south of England. He mainly writes for grown-ups, but as his children have taken no interest in his research into the psychology of religion, he thought he'd try Bible stories instead.

Lauren O'Connell *A Wandering Aramaen*
Lauren is an editor and writer fascinated by the biblical texts, and the stories behind and beyond them. She oversees all things books at The Bible for Normal People, and lives on the lands now called Australia with her husband, kids, and ever-growing flock of chickens.

Carolyn Custis James *Hey There, Stranger*
Carolyn is an award-winning author who thinks deeply about what it means to be a female follower of Jesus. She speaks at churches, Christian colleges, and theological seminaries, and is a consulting editor for Zondervan's Exegetical Commentary Series on the New Testament. She blogs at www. carolyncustisjames.com.

Sarah Shectman *A Family Affair*
Sarah Shectman is the managing editor of the Posen Library of Jewish Culture and Civilization. She holds a Ph.D. in Bible and Ancient Near East from Brandeis University. She is the author or co-editor of several books, including the forthcoming *Bloomsbury Handbook of Religion, Gender, and Sexuality in the Ancient Near East*. Sarah lives in San Francisco.

Rachel Starr *Israel, Is It?*
Rachel Starr is Director of Studies at the Queen's Foundation for Ecumenical Theological Education in Birmingham, England. She completed her doctorate in Buenos Aires, Argentina, researching the impact of theologies of marriage on domestic violence. She writes about reading the Bible as a white woman, the Bible and violence, and Latin American biblical interpretation.

Safwat Marzouk *Here Comes the Dreamer*
Safwat Marzouk is the Associate Professor of Old Testament at Union Presbyterian Seminary and an ordained pastor in the Presbyterian Church. As a Christian Egyptian and migrant to the U.S., he interprets the Bible in ways that are interreligiously and interculturally sensitive seeking God's shalom and justice for the vulnerable and the marginalized.

Chauncey Diego Francisco Handy *Here I Am*
Chauncey Diego Francisco Handy is a Chicano scholar of the Hebrew Bible and Assistant Professor of Religion and Humanities at Reed College in Portland, Oregon, USA. He is an ordained teaching elder in the Presbyterian Church (USA) and enjoys trips to the bakery with his family, hiking, and nice coffee.

Brent A. Strawn *By This They Will Know; Rules to Love By*

Brent is D. Moody Smith Distinguished Professor of Old Testament and
Professor of Law at Duke University and a Senior Fellow in the Center for
the Study of Law and Religion at Emory University. He has written six books,
edited over twenty-five volumes, authored over 250 articles, and is an ordained
elder in the North Georgia Conference of The United Methodist Church.

Mark Brett *Home*

Mark Brett is a white Australian biblical scholar who was raised in Papua
New Guinea. Having taught in Naarm/Melbourne since 1992, his research
has focused on ethnicity, political theology, and decolonial studies. He is
collaborating with Aboriginal and Islander colleagues on the refashioning of
biblical studies in Australia and Oceania.

Erin H. Moon *When Judges Judged*

Erin is the Resident Bible Scholar on the *Faith Adjacent* podcast. She's the
author of *Every Broken Thing*, *O Heavy Lightness*, *Memento Mori*, *Dis/entangle*,
and *Mercy Seat*, and she is also the Senior Creative at the Popcast Media
Group. Erin cares deeply about chips and salsa, as well as creating and caring
for communities of curious, kind people. She lives in Birmingham, Alabama
with her husband, three kids, and dog Bear.

Cynthia Shafer-Elliott *The People Want a King*

Dr. Shafer-Elliott is an Associate Professor of the Hebrew Bible/Old Testament
at Baylor University. An experienced field archaeologist and part of the
excavations at Tel Halif and Tel Abel Beth Maacah, her research emphasizes
household archaeology and issues of religion, gender, food, and social memory.
She is the author of several books including *The 5 Minute Archaeologist in the
Southern Levant*.

Ellen Davis *Every King Needs a Prophet*

Ellen Davis is the Amos Ragan Kearns Distinguished Professor of Bible and
Practical Theology at Duke Divinity School and a grandmother of eight. She
writes and speaks for a wide audience of scholars, clergy, and so-called normal

people, both Jews and Christians, who wonder whether and how the Bible speaks to us in contemporary situations.

Morley van Yperen *Every King Needs a Prophet*

Morley van Yperen is a mother of six, grandmother of three, and Theologian in Residence of Ekklesia Contemporary Ballet all of whom she enjoys exploring the Bible with to discover how hearts, minds, and lives might be shaped to learn to live with each other and the world around us.

Katharine Dell *Proverbial Animal Farm; With Friends Like These*

Katharine Dell is a Professor of Old Testament Literature and Theology in the Faculty of Divinity at the University of Cambridge and a Fellow of St. Catharine's College, Cambridge. Her main academic interests are in the wisdom literature of the Old Testament, but she has also written on biblical theology, environmental ethics, and more.

Dan McClellan *A Kingdom Divided*

Dan McClellan is a public scholar of the Bible and religion. He combats the spread of misinformation about both on social media as @maklelan. He received his Ph.D. from the University of Exeter and specializes in biblical studies, cognitive linguistics, and the cognitive science of religion.

Deborah Winters *Here Comes Trouble*

Deborah Winters is first and foremost a follower of Jesus of Nazareth. While following Jesus, she was ordained in the United Church of Christ, became the Old Testament Professor and Director of the Doctor of Ministry program at Palmer Theological Seminary of Eastern University, and helped start www.GodsPreciousChildren.com.

Jione Havea *You Want Me To Do What?!*

Jione Havea is co-parent for a polycultural daughter and native pastor (Methodist) from Tonga who migrated to the land now known as Australia. Jione loves stories and has learned that a story is made up of many stories so he listens for those other stories as well.

Anna Sieges Beal *Here Comes Trouble…Again*

Anna Sieges Beal is an Old and New Testament professor at Gardner-Webb University and a Nerd in Residence with The Bible for Normal People. She specializes in the Minor Prophets and enjoys thinking about how the Bible came together. In her free time, she likes to eat pizza and watch TV with her family.

Alexiana Fry *For I Know the Plans*

Alexiana Fry is a postdoctorate researcher at the University of Copenhagen, working on a project entitled "Divergent Views of Diaspora." Her interests in migration, trauma, and feminism coincide in much of her work, including her first book, *Trauma Talks in the Hebrew Bible*. She is also a proud pug parent.

Joshua James *Are You There, God?*

Joshua T. James (Ph.D., Fuller Theological Seminary) is one of the pastors of The Restoration Project in Salisbury, Maryland, and an adjunct instructor at the Baptist Seminary of Kentucky. He is the author of *The Storied Ethics of the Thanksgiving Psalms* and *Psalms for Normal People*.

Peter Enns *Days Like These*

Peter Enns (Ph.D., Harvard University) is Abram S. Clemens Professor of Biblical Studies at Eastern University in St. Davids, Pennsylvania, and co-host of *The Bible for Normal People* podcast. He has written numerous books, including *The Bible Tells Me So, The Sin of Certainty,* and *How the Bible Actually Works*.

Steed Vernyl Davidson *Home, Again*

Steed Vernyl Davidson serves as the Executive Director of the Society of Biblical Literature. He is Extraordinary Visiting Professor, Old Testament, Department of Old and New Testament, Stellenbosch University, South Africa.

Aaron Higashi *Who Is In & Who Is Out?*

Dr. Aaron Higashi is an adjunct instructor at Grand Canyon University. He received his Ph.D. in Bible, culture, and hermeneutics with an emphasis in

Hebrew Bible from Chicago Theological Seminary (2021) and shares biblical scholarship at @abhbible on TikTok. Aaron lives in Scottsdale, Arizona with his pediatrician wife and three young daughters, where he does jiu-jitsu, drinks too much coffee, and plays video games.

Havilah Dharamraj *The Faithful Foreign Woman*

Havilah Dharamraj is faculty in the department of Biblical Studies at the South Asia Institute of Advanced Christian Studies in Bangalore, India. Her areas of academic interest are Old Testament narrative, reception-centred intertextuality, and comparative literature conversing biblical texts with the sacred texts of other faiths. She encourages the retrieval of traditional methods of storytelling for use in preaching.

Monica J. Melanchthon *For Such a Time as This*

Monica Melanchthon is an Associate Professor of Hebrew Bible/Old Testament Studies at the Pilgrim Theological College, University of Divinity. Monica has a passion for working with communities, particularly of women, and a love of academic research, teaching, and mentoring. Her most recent publication is the co-edited *Bible Blindspots: Dispersion and Othering.*

Brian Fiu Kolia *In the Lions' Den*

Brian Fiu Kolia is a second-generation Australian-born Samoan. He is a lecturer in the Hebrew Bible at Malua Theological College and holds a Ph.D. from the University of Divinity, Melbourne, Australia. He is interested in reading the text from decolonizing, Pasifika/Moana cultural, and indigenous/native perspectives. More importantly, he is a husband to Tanaria and a father to Elichai.

Shayna Sheinfeld *Even More Trouble*

Shayna Sheinfeld is an assistant professor of religion at Augsburg University (Minneapolis, USA) where she teaches courses on biblical and non-canonical texts. Her research emphasizes the vast diversity of Judaism in antiquity. Sheinfeld is the author of numerous books and articles including *Jewish and Christian Women in the Ancient Mediterranean* with Sara Parks and Meredith J. C. Warren (Routledge 2022).

Sarah Emanuel *On the Road to Damascus*
Sarah Emanuel is Assistant Professor of New Testament Studies at Loyola Marymount University in Los Angeles, CA. She specializes in the Jewish origins of the early Jesus movement, ongoing Jewish-Christian encounters, and the relationship between the Bible and broader cultural trends, including humor.

Isaac T. Soon *The Story Collectors*
Isaac Soon is Assistant Professor of Early Christianity at the University of British Columbia. His work focuses on embodiment in the ancient Mediterranean world especially as related to disability, medicine, gender, and enslavement. His first book, *A Disabled Apostle: Impairment and Disability in the Letters of Paul* was published by Oxford University Press (2023).

Jennifer Garcia Bashaw *Mary's Song; A Mighty Wind*
Jennifer is an Associate Professor of New Testament and Christian Ministry at Campbell University in North Carolina. She has a passion for teaching the Bible and is an ordained American Baptist minister who enjoys preaching as well as training and resourcing pastors. She is the author of *Scapegoats: The Gospel through the Eyes of Victims and John for Normal People*.

Shannon K. Evans *Welcome, Baby Jesus*
Shannon K. Evans is the spirituality and culture editor at the National Catholic Reporter and author of *Feminist Prayers for My Daughter, Rewilding Motherhood,* and *The Mystics Would Like a Word*. Shannon is a speaker, retreat leader, and Jesuit Media Lab instructor. She lives in Iowa with her family and chickens.

Tamice Spencer-Helms *Leading the Way*
Tamice is an author, coach, speaker, and theo-activist. With extensive experience in the nonprofit sector, she empowers clients through innovative training and community-focused initiatives. Tamice is the founder of Sub:Culture Inc. an education and equity nonprofit designed to Clear The Path for Black College Students, and the author of *Faith Unleavened: The Wilderness Between Trayvon Martin and George Floyd*.

Shane Claiborne *The Sermon on the Mount; Hey There, Neighbor*
Shane is a prominent speaker, activist, and best-selling author. Founder of The Simple Way, he heads up Red Letter Christians, a movement of folks who are committed to living "as if Jesus meant the things he said." Shane is the author of several books and, in 2023, received the prestigious The King Center's Beloved Community Award for Social Justice from Dr. Bernice King.

Elizabeth Enns Petters *Seeing Jesus*
Lizz is an author and co-host of the *Deconstructing Mamas* podcast. She is deeply passionate about creating a space for spiritual misfits to find a sense of safety and belonging on their faith journeys. She lives with her husband and two young children in Pennsylvania, USA.

Kylie Crabbe *Through the Roof*
Kylie Crabbe is an Associate Professor in the Biblical and Early Christian Studies program at Australian Catholic University and a Uniting Church Minister. Currently, she is working on a major project about disability in early Christianity, and looking especially at how biblical passages about disability have been interpreted in different historical periods—including diverse contemporary settings.

Summer Kinard *Get Up!*
Summer Kinard, M.Div., Th.M., an autistic Orthodox Christian theologian, and mother of five, writes and leads vibrant interactive workshops that combine depth of prayerful study on Christ's Incarnation and deep listening to help everyone participate in our Loving-kind God. She is the author of several books and writes regularly on her substack Some Myrrh and summerkinard.com.

Jennifer T. Kaalund *By A Well*
Jennifer T. Kaalund (Ph.D., New Testament and Early Christianity, Drew University) is an independent scholar. Her research focuses on contextual Biblical hermeneutics, material culture, and African American culture. She is the author of *Reading Hebrews and 1 Peter with the African American Great Migration: Diaspora, Place, and Identity* (Bloomsbury T&T Clark Press, 2018).

Meredith J. C. Warren *They Were Satisfied*

Dr. Meredith J. C. Warren is a Senior Lecturer in Biblical and Religious Studies at the University of Sheffield. She is the author of numerous books and articles on gender in early Christianity, food and meals in ancient literature, and anti-Judaism and the New Testament. Her most recent book is *Jewish and Christian Women in the Ancient Mediterranean* with Shayna Sheinfeld and Sara Parks (Routledge 2022).

Camille Szramiak Arneberg *What Kind of Man?*

Camille is mom to two wonderful kids, and holds an M.S. in Communication from Boston University and a Certificate in Youth and Theology from Princeton Theological Seminary. Her deepest desire is to see experiential encounters with God's love move people to peace—with themselves, the world, and each other. She currently resides in Austin, Texas.

Marika Rose *What Is Better?*

Dr Marika Rose is a senior lecturer in philosophical theology at the University of Winchester. She is the author of *A Theology of Failure: Žižek Against Christian Innocence* (Fordham University Press, 2019) and *Theology for the End of the World* (SCM Press, 2023).

Savannah Locke *Rejoice with Me*

Savannah is a writer exploring the intersections of faith, life, and beauty. With a Master's degree in Anabaptist studies, she is shaped by the rich heritage of peacemaking and aims to expand that peace through her work. Based just outside Nashville, TN, Savannah lives with her husband, Todd, and their two dogs, Bentley and Prudence.

Miguel A. De La Torre *It Ain't Fair*

Dr. Miguel A. De La Torre is an international scholar, documentarian, novelist, academic author, and scholar activist. Since obtaining his doctoral degree in 1999, he has authored over a hundred articles and published forty-seven books, six of which won national awards. He presently serves as Professor of Social Ethics and Latinx Studies at the Iliff School of Theology in Denver.

Raj Nadella *Making Things Right*

Dr. Raj Nadella is the Samuel A. Cartledge Associate Professor of New Testament at Columbia Theological Seminary. Nadella is the author of *Dialogue Not Dogma: Many Voices in the Gospel of Luke* (Bloomsbury, 2011) and co-editor of *Christianity and the Law of Migration* (Routledge, 2021). Nadella has written for publications such as *The Christian Century, The Huffington Post*, and *Sojourners*.

Richard Rohr *A Very Big Party*

Richard Rohr is a globally recognized Franciscan friar and ecumenical teacher whose work bears witness to the deep wisdom of Christian mysticism. He is the founder of the Center for Action and Contemplation in Albuquerque, New Mexico, an educational nonprofit that introduces spiritual seekers to the Christian contemplative path of transformation. He is the author of many books.

Jarrod McKenna *A Funny Kind of King*

Jarrod is an award-winning peace activist committed to seeing the transfiguring fire of God's love become our experience in prayer and our program for ecological and social healing. Husband to Kathleen and father to Tyson, Winni, Hugo, Noah, and Gough, Jarrod is the co-host of *Inverse Podcast*, teaching pastor at Steeple Church and Founding Director of CommonGrace. org.au. He lives and worships on Noongar Boodja country, found on maps as Perth, Australia.

Marlena Graves *Do This & Remember*

Marlena Graves is the Assistant Professor of Spiritual Formation at Northeastern Seminary on the campus of Roberts Wesleyan University in Rochester, NY. She has written five books and over two hundred articles for a variety of venues like *Christianity Today*, *Relevant*, *Sojourners*, and more. She is married to Shawn and has three brilliant growing girls. She hopes to leave a little bit of shalom in her wake.

Bradley Jersak *Gethsemane*
Bradley Jersak is an author and teacher based in Abbotsford, BC. He serves as the Principal of St. Stephen's University (SSU.ca) in New Brunswick, where he continues as the Director and faculty member of SSU's School of Theology & Culture. He also teaches peace studies courses with JFI.SSU.ca and is a regular speaker with the Open Table Conference crew. He writes regularly for the *Clarion Journal* and *CWR* magazine.

Drew G. I. Hart *My God, My God*
Drew G. I. Hart is an Associate Professor of Theology at Messiah University where he directs the Thriving Together: Congregations for Racial Justice program. He co-hosts *Inverse Podcast*, is the author of several books, and co-edited *Reparations and the Theological Disciplines: Prophetic Voices for Remembrance, Reckoning, and Repair.* Drew is married to Renee and is the father of three sons.

Elizabeth Schrader Polczer *Do Not Be Afraid*
Elizabeth "Libbie" Schrader Polczer is an Assistant Professor of New Testament at Villanova University. Her studies focus on textual criticism, Mary Magdalene, and the Gospel of John. Elizabeth transitioned to religious scholarship after a long career as a singer/songwriter. Her research has been featured in *The Daily Beast, Christian Century*, and the *National Catholic Reporter.*

Rachel Mann *Everyone's Invited!*
Rachel Mann is a UK-based priest, poet, scholar and broadcaster. She has written fifteen books and contributed to many more. She writes regularly for *The Christian Century* and *The Church Times* and is a regular broadcaster on BBC radio. She is the first out trans woman to hold a senior role in the Church of England.

Terry J. Stokes *A Revelation*
Terry J. Stokes served in parish ministry for several years before moving into his current nonprofit community development work in central New Jersey. He is the author of *Prayers for the People* (Convergent 2021) and *Jesus and the Abolitionists: How Anarchist Christianity Empowers the People* (Broadleaf 2024).

Randy Woodley *A New Heaven and A New Earth*
Randy Woodley is an author, speaker, activist and wisdom-keeper. He is Co-Sustainer at Eloheh Indigenous Center for Earth Justice and Professor of Faith and Culture Emeritus, Portland Seminary. Several of his books include *Becoming Rooted*, *Journey to Eloheh* and *Shalom and the Community of Creation*.

THIS BOOK

Publishing Director Lauren O'Connell

Consulting Scholars Peter Enns, Amy-Jill Levine

Development Camille Szramiak Arneberg

Design & Layout Ellie Boultwood

Proofreading Brittany Prescott Hodge

Thanks to Sarah Anderson, Jared Byas, Jennifer Garcia Bashaw, Darren Kizer, Savannah Locke, Karen Peazzoni, Katie Perrott, Nikki Pierce, Cynthia Shafer-Elliott, Anna Sieges Beal, Bekah Sine, Isaac T. Soon, Danny Wong, Melissa Yandow

A very special thanks to the many children who listened to our stories, gave us their feedback by laughing in all the right–and wrong!–places, asking us the tough questions, and showing us how to read the Bible through a child's eyes. We couldn't do what we do without you:

Lyric Ansell; Asher Arneberg; Ava Arneberg; Cohen Attard; Lewis Attard; Ivan Badenhorst; Otto Badenhorst; Sarah Bayer; Bramble Beal; Emmy Beal; Wren Bell; Charlie Clay; Ella-Rose Clay; Malachi Dacre-Davis; Eleanor Dievendorf; Enoch Dievendorf; Silas Dievendorf; Alice Fillbrook; Charlotte Fillbrook; Ebenezer Files; Malachi Files; Moses Files; Simeon Files; Jubilee Freeman; Leo Freeman; Perry Freeman; Roger Freeman; Stevie Freeman; Zion Freeman; Emmett Gard; Josie Gard; Iliana Graves; Valentina Graves; Isabella Graves; Diya Lākai Havea; Amira, Aria, and Addi; Caden Jackson; Emma Jackson; Kate Janz; Faith Jensen; Jacqueline Jensen; Rose Jensen; Clare Lam; Judah Lam; Lucy Lau; Zoe Leach; Kai Lewis; Peyton Lewis; Zoe Lewis; Briar Mann; August Mann; Avery Maxson; Elijah Maxson; Liliana Maxson; Izzy Neal; Kaycee Neal; Tilly Neal; Tripp Neal; Aiden Nixon; Zach Nixon; Hannah O'Connell; Maggie O'Connell; Rosie O'Connell; András Papp; Harlym Spencer-Helms; Ben Thompson; Isla Thompson; Ezra Wilkinson; Wim Wilkinson; Adelyn Woods; Eden Woods; Aliyah and Samira; Asher VB; Aynsley, Gavriel, Eliana, and Sofia; Des, Toby, Q, and Finney; Harper, Virginia, Jude, and Hosanna; Peter, Ender, and Emmett; Scott and Amos

Want even more great content?

Head over to **thebiblefornormalpeople.com** where you can find tons of resources to help you explore the Bible.

CLASSES

Study the Bible's origins, influences, and themes online in your own time.

BOOKS

Read accessible, engaging Bible commentaries written by scholars just for you.

PODCASTS

Listen to hundreds of conversations about faith and the Bible.

COMMUNITY

Join the **Society of Normal People** and get access to:

- All of our classes
- Exclusive Q&As with our team and biblical scholars
- Ad-free podcast stream
- Sneak peeks at upcoming projects
- A thriving online community of people who are curious about the Bible.

For more The Bible for Normal People content, sign up for our newsletter or follow us on socials @thebiblefornormalpeople.